"This book couldn't come at a more poignant time. With everything going on in our world we need Charles's powerful story of redemption and hope. This book is an incredible reminder that even when the world gives up on people God never does. Charles has also been a mentor of mine for over a decade and I can say that the wisdom he has comes from God. Not only is his story incredible but the man behind the book is one of the most amazing human beings I've ever met. I hope you enjoy Made Clean and share it with those who need to be reminded of hope!"

Nolan Lee
Pastor
Award-winning Artist & Illustrator

"The story of Charles Lee Knuckles is remarkable. I literally feel like I've had a front-row seat to his life. This hidden gem of wisdom is not only worth reading but worth living by. At times, I found myself lost in the story of pain, heartache, and triumph. I am thankful for this story. It's men like Charles that give me hope that Jesus is still in the business of handpicking lives for the express purpose of magnifying the goodness of God."

Myron Pierce
Pastor
Founder, Village Social

"His raw, engaging story intermixed with profound biblical counsel is a perfect read for those on their way to sobriety, those in the struggle to stay sober, and those who care about their friends being damaged by addiction."

Barney Wiget
Author, *Reaching Rahab*

"Charles is a remarkable man who has led an extraordinary life. His story is one of impossible pain and unimaginable loss, but it's also one of unimaginable restoration and impossible redemption. It's the kind of story that is only available through radical surrender to a good and almighty God. Charles captivates live audiences with his testimony. His vulnerability and humility and insight never fail to bring surprise and tears and laughter. Fortunately for those who have not been able to catch him live, Charles heard God's invitation to write his story down and offer his hard-fought wisdom in the form of this precious volume. Through his words, many lives will be saved. I pray that you open these pages and discover just what God has for you here."

Justin Camp
Author, *The WiRE Series for Men*
Co-Founder, Gather Ministries

MADE CLEAN

THE TRUE STORY OF A MAN'S SPIRITUAL
AWAKENING FROM THE OPPRESSIVE GRIP
OF DESTITUTION AND ADDICTION

CHARLES LEE
KNUCKLES

KMG PUBLISHING

Made Clean

Print ISBN: 9781732116450

eBook ISBN: 9781732116443

Copyright © 2021 Charles Lee Knuckles

www.charlesknuckles.com

Editorial Work: Rachel Rant

Cover Design: arté digital graphics

Interior Layout: Aaron Snethen

Published by KMG Publishing

DEDICATION

This book is dedicated to my beautiful sister Nellie Mae Knuckles Lawrence. She is my hero. She lived the same hard life in poverty I did, but she did it in much better fashion. Although she was a small female in stature, she was strong in courage. She left our last foster home when she was fifteen. She was married to one man and had three children. She worked as an Employment Specialist for the Archdiocese of Philadelphia, helping young people with Down Syndrome get and keep jobs. She loved God, she loved her family, she loved people, and she loved life. This is for Nellie—a loving mother, wife, sister, and grandmother.

PREFACE

In this book, I am trying to bring people together through very trying and tragic issues in our society. I believe my story, what I have learned, and what I teach others will help bridge racial and social divides through greater understanding. Not only did I live through the worst that society could do to a child and adult, but I was set free.

After 30-plus years of slavery to chronic addiction and homelessness, unspeakable abuse, and poverty, I finally found my voice. In this book, I will show you what happens when I didn't follow God's lead, what happened when I did, and where God took me.

So, I will speak to you as a rescued and recovered addict—and as a clinician and mentor who strives to show others the path to freedom.

I will speak to you as a man of deep faith in God. A God who longs to rescue all of us. The only grace I could give others was the grace I had received from God when I received Jesus as my Lord and Savior. I was a terrible sinner, as lost as a man could be, and He reached down from Heaven, brought me to that Christian rehab center, and saved me. I knew the miraculous hand of grace in my life was the hand of

Jesus. After that, I was compelled to work hard at telling others of His miraculous hand of grace.

I will give you tools to maximize the effectiveness of your life. You don't have to be homeless; many people live in mansions but have homeless hearts. You don't have to be addicted to drugs or alcohol; many people are addicted and have not been paying attention. Anyone can utilize these spiritual tools and get something out of this book to help them in life. These spiritual tools are for everybody. God has long since laid out the path, even if you have yet to do the footwork.

This is the story of how I became the man I am today—faithful, helpful, joyful—and free!

PART ONE: MY STORY

CHAPTER ONE
DIFFERENT AND UNLOVABLE

When I was growing up, I was considered different. I was called a "Negro" and a "colored boy." Back then, that was the acceptable description of someone like me. I've always been partial to "colored people" myself. To me, "colored people" was a better description and left a measure of dignity. "Negro," on the other hand, seemed void of anything that resembled any sense of pride. The other nice thing about being called "colored people" was that, deep down, I knew all people were colored something. So, the term brought about a sort of secret equality in my mind.

I was born in 1949 in Philadelphia, Pennsylvania. Immediately, I learned the ground rules of the two worlds around me: the world of colored people and the world of white people. These worlds were segregated yet strangely dependent on each other. I don't remember seeing too many white people back then, except those in positions of authority, like policemen and store owners. I don't remember talking to a white person in my early childhood.

Two years after my birth, my sister was born. Shortly after, my mom caught a cold, and with no medical treatment and no heat, it turned into deadly pneumonia. She should not have died, but colored people could not afford medical care, and they were not allowed in many hospitals. Mom was only thirty when she died. I grew up fearing turning thirty, thinking I had a good chance of dying at that age as well.

Most white people considered my sister and me as less than human. Mom was a poor lady from South Carolina, we were told. I don't know what made her move to the city. Viola O'Neal was her name. Because she died when I was only two years old, I never really knew her. I have two pictures of her that my sister saved over the years. I often gaze into the pictures to see what I can tell about her. One picture is just a headshot, but the other shows my mom, sister, and me on a small street. It's a winter day, and my sister is in her arms, all bundled up. I have a winter outfit on, but Mom is just wearing a flimsy jacket, as if she couldn't afford a heavy coat. It looks so cold that I can't help but cry for her.

I never knew my father, but I took his last name. To this day, I don't know what he looks like. I have no pictures or anything like that. I wouldn't recognize him if he were in the room with me. Often, as a child, whenever I would see older men on the streets, on a bus, or in a store, I would look at them and wonder—*Are you my daddy?* I constantly wondered what I had done to make me so unlovable. Why was I unwanted? Why would a father not stay around to get to know his son? What was wrong with me? Would no one ever like me or love me?

My sister and I ended up in an orphanage, and we were told they wanted to separate us because it would increase the possibility of adoption. Apparently, because my sister would cry so loudly every time the workers would take me out of the room, they finally relented and kept us together. I was too young to remember any of this. Later, a social worker told us this story, and I've always wanted to think it was true. I do know that adoption never happened for us. I don't know why. I guess that for poverty-stricken people, fostering was lucrative. A paycheck seemed to be the only reason people would take us into their homes.

This upbringing is how my identity was shaped and formed: around mystery, feeling "less than" because I was colored, the absence of parents, and the pervading sense of being unlovable and not belonging anywhere. This was how I saw myself.

CHAPTER TWO
CHILDHOOD TERROR

My earliest memories were of being beaten, starved, neglected, and abused in poverty-stricken foster homes with people who cared more about the government check than the kids placed in their care. Some memories I blocked out, because it's very hard to survive thinking about those things. Memories of the hurt and pain, the dreams destroyed—often literally beat out of me by foster parents, street thugs, and bullies. I was haunted by thoughts like: *What happened to me? Why did they do that to me?*

I learned to adapt to the beatings, the hunger, and even molestation. Still, the trauma left the most profound imprint on my psyche and the most vivid of memories. I was in survival mode my whole childhood. What I didn't know is that I would carry these wounds into adulthood, and they would affect how I lived. My emotions were crippled by these deep wounds that seemed to define me. I wanted someone to love me, but I saw myself as unlovable. No matter how deeply I would love someone, eventually, I would sabotage the relationship—thinking that they deserved better and I could never be good enough.

I was also hungry all the time, which got me into trouble. Once, at a foster home, there seemed to be some sort of party for the adults. They were all laughing loudly and drinking, having a good time, when a careless foster parent placed a boney fish in front of me for dinner. I'd never eaten fried fish before, so no one had shown me how to eat fish with bones. Starving, I started wolfing it down. I choked on a big bone and could not breathe. I remember being at the top of a stairwell choking, gasping for breath, feeling utterly helpless. No one helped me; as a matter of fact, all the drunk adults laughed even louder than before. I don't know how the bone got out, but I do know that I didn't eat fish for the next 20 years, no matter how hungry I was!

Now I know wonderful, kind, and caring foster parents exist. Mine weren't them. I vividly remember being told by one of my foster parents, "You're not our kids anyway. You're here because nobody else wants you. As a matter of fact, nobody cares what we do to you."

One foster parent insisted we call her "Big Mama" and used to say, "If I don't like what happens here, it's back to the orphanage before you can blink." The whole "before you can blink" thing struck fear into my young heart. I would literally try not to blink! When I saw an episode of *I Dream of Jeannie* for the first time, Jeannie's blink would remind me of Big Mama's threats—even though Big Mama and Jeannie looked nothing alike! I was beyond well-behaved back then, so I could never watch *I Dream of Jeannie* without a certain dread. I lived in fear of doing something wrong, but it seemed I couldn't do anything right.

No matter how well I acted, my foster parents renounced me as surely as the winters were cold and meals were grim. Sitting in the orphanage between foster homes, I was surrounded by kids and noise. There were people around me, but I felt utterly alone. I was scared of every shadow. My imagination would conjure up frightening images through the frosted panes of glass that separated the rooms of the orphanage. Since the frosted glass was everywhere, I couldn't escape my fear. My young imagination scared me with every shadow and image. I knew that I was not safe. Nowhere was safe, and often that fear proved to be true.

The orphanage was a cold, scary place of concrete and steel. The only escape was on the black steel fire escape at the back of the building. But if you got caught alone there by some creepy older kid, bad things would happen. It was no place for a young child. Yet, it was the only place that felt at all safe. We abandoned kids fought, stole, and were touched inappropriately. We accepted this as our reality, and there was nothing we could do about it. Some of the monsters that appeared through the frosted glass panes were not imaginary; they were real. They were older kids and often the adults we were supposed to trust.

AM I WORTH IT?

At seven and eight years old, in a foster home, I endured repeated sexual assaults and encounters. It seemed that every kid in the neighborhood was aware of sex. They acted out what they learned from adults on a daily basis. There were more sexual assaults than I want to say. Around this time, an older man forced me to have oral sex, tears running down my face. I don't remember crying after that day. I would make sounds like crying to try to stop the beatings from my foster parents. But the louder I would yell in pain, the more it seemed to please them, and there were no tears. It was as if a part of me dried up and died.

I just wanted to be like some of the kids I would see on TV. They seemed happy, and I desperately wanted to know happy. It would be wonderful to be ordinary, doing ordinary kid things, with normal parents who loved and cared for me. In my imaginary world, my parents would not beat me unmercifully, and they certainly wouldn't abuse me sexually. In my fictional world, I would never be forced to do things I didn't want to do.

When I was ten years old, the eighteen-year-old girl who babysat us forced me to have sexual intercourse with her every time she worked for our foster parents. One time while she was raping me, I peed in the bed and made her mad. She was frantic to get the sheets clean by the time the adults returned. I received a terrible beating for the wet bed, but I was too afraid to tell on the babysitter.

I believed I was not worth rescuing, that what my foster parents told me was true: "Nobody cares about you or cares what we do to you, and you better not tell the caseworker."

No one was there to say, "Don't do that to that child. It's not right."

Inside, I would say to myself, "Whatever you do to me, I will survive."

I know these accounts may be a bit graphic for some people, but I hope I have been descriptive enough for you to feel the pain and understand the deep wounds of a child who lived in constant fear. Every time the door closed behind me, whoever the predator was, I felt fear and confusion surge through my young body and mind. I was in fight or flight mode so often, but I could not fight or take flight. My brain simply started to shut down all emotions, all hope. I just wanted to be a normal kid, but there was no normalcy for me.

As adults in our fifties, my sister and I got together one day and visited the orphanage in North Philadelphia. It was much more modern than what we remembered. We walked in together, and I can't imagine what they thought of us. We identified ourselves and asked if we could see our records. To our surprise, one of the workers brought a stack of files out and directed us to a huge magnifying glass. They still had our records on old microfiche sheets. We put one after another under the magnifier and tearfully read caseworkers' notes about us in the early 1950s.

One wrote, "Charles' and his sister's legs still wobble when they walk. The children are malnourished." Another remarked, "Teacher reported to me that Charles was sent home from kindergarten because he smelled like urine." Still, another reported, "marks from beatings are all over his body." We read as much as we could, trying not to cry too loudly. Finally, we had to stop because it was too much. We thanked them and left.

We didn't talk much during the ride back. We never spoke about that visit again, and my sister has since passed away.

Culture of Violence

I am confident that the violence and neglect I experienced as a child were partially symptoms of abject poverty—the severe deprivation of basic human rights and necessities. Poverty spawns a volatile mix of alcohol, drugs, illegal guns, and lack of hope, urging people to turn on each other in desperate, perverse, and cruel ways. Only 16 percent of children growing up in these harsh ghettos escape into something better. This was the reality of my growing-up years, and it was a nightmare most of the time.

The ability to explode into epic violence seems to be a common and valuable attribute in poor neighborhoods. The willingness to take things to the level of permanent injury and even murder shapes the fear of and respect for gangsters from those who must live around them. Fifty percent of law is from the gangs, and fifty percent is from police and judges—either can kill you. For all of us who lived in places of violence, fear shaped our lives. Make no mistake; this was slavery! There is little freedom in bad neighborhoods, and predators at every turn. From the alphas to the survivors, anxiety ordered our daily patterns and ruled our lives. While it was advantageous to be an alpha, I saw myself as a survivor because I could still dream.

I had no desire to hone any of the violent skill sets I witnessed. I didn't hang out with gang members, nor did I join a gang. I didn't like the practice of imposing fear and intimidation on others like I'd seen and experienced. Instead, I tried to avoid these tactics. They were horrifying. I don't know why, but something inside of me knew the world I lived in was not right.

I admired and marveled at people who were different. I was attracted to those people called "nerds" or "squares" back in the day. I think I was drawn to these kids because they were adventurers. They had vivid imaginations, and we had fun.

I had a few friends who were considered oddballs like me, and I was loyal to them. If someone wanted me to fight, all they had to do was mess with my friends. I wasn't as quick to defend myself, but if you messed with my friends, you'd have real trouble on your hands—or at least as much as I could muster!

None of us guys were real fighters. We could fight, but we weren't deadly. We had no desire to harm anyone. My friends were gifted in music and literature, but we all had to hide our gifts in our neighborhood. Unless you had a big family to protect you, you did not want to be the smart or talented guy. Kids like that annoyed the gangsters. For Al, Jimmy, Little Mikey, and me, we had to be family for each other to survive the streets of Philly.

Despite my constant malnourishment, I developed into a strong young boy and a fast runner. I often had to run. It wouldn't be until much later that I would discover that I could fight in a cinch too. Refusing to join a gang when invited had heavy consequences, especially when you didn't have parents or an older brother to protect you. I paid that price, and I was hunted by individuals from gangs almost daily.

Going to school was like running the gauntlet full of deadly traps. As a dreamer, I tried to turn this into an imaginary adventure. And it was imaginary—until it wasn't. Sometimes, despite my efforts to avoid them, I was jumped and beaten after school by bullies. because, even though we went to school at different times in the morning, we all left at the same time. When that bell rang, I prepared for what would happen next.

Little Tommy was the leader of a gang called "The Moon." Because they were elementary school students, they were often referred to as the "Peewee Squad. Tommy and his boys would be waiting at the school gate or the corner. They were always trying to prove that they could be just as vicious as the Moon Juniors, who were teenagers that had the reputation of doing the hard or wet work for the gang. They carried drugs and weapons because, as minors, they received lesser sentences if caught.

The Peewee Squad was always looking for a victim to get their street cred, and they had their sights set on me. Sometimes, I could get enough speed to fly right past them before they realized it was me. Other times, they were prepared for that tactic and would catch me. Little Tommy would show off in front of his gang by slapping me in the face and punching me in the stomach. The goal was to punch someone in the stomach so hard that they would puke. It would frustrate Tommy when he couldn't make me puke. I would stand there and let him shame me and laugh. Eventually, he would let me go with a stream of profanities and name-calling.

One day, Tommy hit me real hard, but this time I fought back. I couldn't believe it—I was winning! To my amazement, I was stronger and faster than Tommy. Unfortunately, seeing that I was about to win, his gang jumped in and tried to get me down so they could stomp and kick me. Somehow, I got away. You never wanted to let them get you down on the ground—because you might never get back up.

My next encounter with Little Tommy was different. On Monday in class, I could see a new look in his eyes. More than his typical evil look, it was piercing, and he was laser-beam focused on me. When school got out, the crowd was bigger than usual. There seemed to be electric anticipation in the air, like something big was about to happen. I knew I couldn't break through with a running start this time because the crowd was too dense. I walked out of the school, and just as I got to the street, out popped Little Tommy. This time, he was armed with a baseball bat.

Tommy swung the bat hard, hitting me in the head just above the left eye. I still carry the scar. Everything started spinning. Even though I couldn't think, and I could barely see through the curtain of blood that ran down my eyes, instinctively, I knew falling would mean death. I flashed back to the first time I saw this happen in first grade. We were in the schoolyard when a gang chased a guy down and killed him right in front of us during recess. Now, I was that guy.

Somehow, even with everything spinning and lights flashing in my head, my legs started running, zigzagging in and out between parked cars, not letting Tommy set up for the kill swing. Finally, I ran up to a crossing guard, blood streaming down my face, and cried out, "They are trying to kill me!"

He said, "Run, kid! There's nothing I can do. Run!" He didn't want to become a victim too. I don't know how, but I was able to get away that day. When I got home, my foster parents fussed at me for getting blood everywhere. They took me to the doctor, and I got a bunch of stitches over my left eye. My foster parents were angry and blamed the whole thing on me, complaining that I was a mess they were expected to clean up. They didn't report the assault to the police, nor did they go to school with me or do any of the things good parents would have done. They made it clear that even in my brush with death, I was an unwanted burden to them. I was on my own.

That deadly assault seemed to satisfy Tommy's thirst for my blood for a while. I think in his mind, he figured he owned me again, and he did in a sense. I was terrorized by the level of violence he and his gang were capable of, and I knew I could not possibly match it. The next time I saw him, my head was still bandaged, and my face was still swollen. He laughed at me and asked if I wanted some more. I had no stomach for retribution. I learned a valuable lesson that day: avoid psychopaths. Unfortunately, that was impossible in my neighborhood. I would have to learn about violence and when to use it.

THE SHADOW OF MALNUTRITION

You can look at a child and know immediately if they aren't getting enough to eat or are eating all the wrong foods. There is a shadow of deprivation on their faces. More than 13 million kids in America go hungry or live in homes where food is not nutritious.

There is evidence that sweet foods are linked to reward centers in the brain, which is why some people turn to them for comfort in times of stress, like living in the ghetto. Food with high sugar and fat content can be like a mini-vacation from the high-stress and cramped existence of the ghetto, but the vacation is short-lived and can shorten your life. In combination with a lack of nutrition, these unhealthy foods can harm the ability to learn and compete in academia. When there is no supermarket in your neighborhood and transportation is not available, you eat cheap food. Cheap food is usually bad food, but for me and all the other hungry kids, there was no other recourse.

I don't know how many millions of kids were hungry when I was a kid, but I know that I was one of them. In my old neighborhood, every street corner had a little mom-and-pop store. In New York, they are called bodegas; in Philly, they are called corner stores. We bought our food from these little stores, from street-hustler trucks, or out of the trunk of someone's car. The choices were limited, and the prices varied, but they were a lifesaver in our neighborhoods.

Since there was no food at my foster home, I had to occasionally steal food after school. I was starved and severely malnourished at different points in my childhood, so I was willing to do almost anything for food. One day, I was chased out of the streetcar barn for eating road salt from the pile. It was an enormous pile of salt, a stash for snow days. I thought I had hit the jackpot until an angry worker kicked me out with a stern warning.

On my way home from school, as casually as I could, I would watch the corner store merchant as he worked on his fruits and vegetables outside. I tried my best to be incognito. When he took a customer inside, I would don *The Flash* persona. Running as fast as I could, I'd grab a big Red Delicious apple in midstride and continue running until I felt safe. I knew *The Flash* didn't steal, and I had a problem with that thought, but my rationale was that he was never starved, and I was.

There was a popular urban superstition that when running to get away, you were uncatchable once you turned the nearest corner. It was nonsense, but we believed it so much that pursuers often would give up the chase at the corner. If he saw me as I ran away, the store owner would yell, "You little street urchin!" Later, I found out what that meant. I also found out that the man was an Italian immigrant and knew I was hungry. He had seen me eating scraps off the ground and out of his trashcan, and he felt compassion for me. He probably would have given me an apple if I had found the courage to ask him.

The Red Delicious apple made an excellent meal for my sister and me, sitting in the kitchen playing imaginary food games. Our foster parents were rarely there after school, and there was no food for us. If there was food in the fridge, we weren't allowed to touch it. We didn't think anything of taking turns passing the apple back and forth to each other. We imagined that the next bite was a burger or hotdog.

We developed gourmet imaginations even though we had never tasted anything remotely gourmet!

In junior high school, I got a job working for a Greek immigrant, making cheesesteaks and hoagies. It didn't pay much money, but Mr. Jimmy was happy to feed me! He was a very nice guy. We had great conversations about what I was learning, and I loved his Greek accent and hearty laugh.

Even so, at a very young age, I had become a thief and a liar. When I asked for food, clothing, or some money, my foster parents would beat me. It was easier and much less painful to steal what I needed. I stole a slice of bread when Big Mama wasn't looking and hid behind the sofa to have an imaginary gourmet feast. If there was peanut butter, I would carefully scoop it out without clinking the butter knife against the jar. Then I would sneak into a corner and scarf it down before anyone noticed.

There is a technique to eating a dry peanut butter sandwich. I had to take tiny bites so the sandwich wouldn't choke up in my throat. We called dry peanut butter sandwiches "choke sandwiches." Sometimes, I would imagine the bread had both peanut butter *and* jelly on it, although jelly was rarely in the house.

Some foster kids who had been in a foster home longer had a warped relationship with the foster parents and would delight in seeing the newer kids get beaten. If they caught me with stolen food, they would say, "Ooooooh, I'm gonna tell! Ooooooh, you are gonna get a whooping!" And sure enough, I would get that whipping while my foster siblings had a good laugh. By telling on me, they would be rewarded with a special bond or closeness, a little more food, or special privileges. As I look back, it's hard to fault them. Like me, they were just trying to survive.

I watched other kids who were not hungry. They had clean, up-to-date clothing and toys. I didn't own a single toy until we took a trip downtown when I was about seven. We walked around a department store, and I wandered into the toy department. I saw a ray gun that looked like one in a *Buck Rogers* adventure. I picked it up and started running around the store, making zapping noises and pointing the ray gun at everything I could. Then, when it was time to go, I walked right out of the store with the ray gun.

At first, the other kids were delighted and had fun zapping and getting zapped with me. But, when we got back to Big Mama's house, it was a different story. One of the older kids told her I had the ray gun. Without a word, Big Mama took the gun from me and gave it to him. I remember thinking, "They're never going to let me have anything." But I would go on to steal anything I needed or wanted any chance I got. In my mind, it was the only way I would have anything.

TREASURES AND FRIENDS

Since I was the kid with the crazy foster parents, it was hard to find friends whose parents would let them hang out with me. Al and Jimmy were my best friends. Their parents would only tolerate small doses of my company, so I was usually invited over when their parents weren't home. Al and Jimmy were both gifted, Al in music and Jimmy in writing songs and poetry. Both Jimmy and Al sang well, but I couldn't carry a tune. I can remember Jimmy singing and moving to the rhythm. His poetry was powerful, dramatic, and sometimes funny. When Al played his saxophone, the whole block listened. Everybody knew he was talented.

Then there was Little Mikey, who would barely speak up. I knew I had to protect him as best I could. He was so little, and he'd been bullied so much that he was timid unless he was with our group. I always thought I brought very little to the table except for my imagination, loyalty, and admiration for them all. We had lively conversations despite where we lived and what was going on in our neighborhood.

We all had our favorite superheroes, and mine was *The Flash*. I liked the idea of a parallel universe, like a second Earth reality. My Earth reality was unbearable, so I always dreamed of a better one. Like so many people stuck in poverty, I had a prolific dream life because my reality was so horrible. I let my imagination run wild with stories like *The Flash*. Something deep inside me still believed my dreams were attainable. I just had to keep hoping and pushing through.

Another reason I was into *The Flash* was that he is very fast. I thought that maybe if I ran fast enough, I could escape the ugly reality in which I existed just like he did. Like *The Flash*, I was very fast and tried to outrun the dangers surrounding me. When I was running at full speed, the ugliness around me became a blur. Before a hustler or a pervert could get the words, "Hey kid," out of their mouth, most times I would be a half-block away. Reading about *The Flash* helped me to experience moments where my childhood terrors disappeared, and as I ran like *The Flash* through my neighborhood for a few brief seconds, I was safe.

I don't remember how many foster homes in which my sister and I lived. Sometime after Big Mama's house, we landed in the house of a couple of partygoers. One of my special privileges was going out at night, around 9 p.m., and collecting papers to be recycled. The money went to my foster parents to support their party habit. I was nine years old when I was given this "special privilege." I had to pull a little wagon through the neighborhood and go through people's trash to collect old newspapers and magazines. I was used to trash-picking, but the scary part was the dark of night. I was already afraid of monsters in the daytime, so I was doubly scared of monsters at night. However, the thought of disobeying my foster dad was even more frightening.

Although I was afraid, I decided to make my trash-picking an adventure. I soon discovered that I didn't have to focus only on newspapers. There were other treasures in the trash. One night I found a whole stack of *Doc Savage* paperbacks, written in the 1940s. I loved reading those novelettes. They would fuel my imagination, and I had a new superhero to emulate. Late at night, after stacking the newspapers for my foster father as fast as I could, I would read chapter after chapter until I fell asleep. I had to hide the books in my secret hiding place so my foster father would not sell them.

One night, one of my mysterious trashcan benefactors put two novels in the trash that would change the way I saw the world forever: *The Adventures of Tom Sawyer* and *The Adventures of Huckleberry Finn*. Huckleberry Finn was my favorite. His adventures, like mine, had strong elements of danger, and he always found a way to escape certain doom.

I would go on to read books like *Treasure Island*, *Peter Pan*, *The Prince and the Pauper*, and *Oliver Twist*. My books became my treasures! They helped me escape and taught me how to be a boy while enduring a hard childhood. I would retreat into my secret world of books—of heroes, mysteries, and adventures—and my hunger pains and fears would subside. I had secret smiles no one knew, and for a short time, I would not be in the ghetto anymore. Maybe I would be on the banks of the Mississippi River or other places I only saw in my imagination. In this way, I lived a double life, and now it was more than just survival; it was high adventure!

My clandestine, late-night reading expanded my ever-growing list of superheroes and aided my imagination to soar to new heights. I would run like the wind in the way of Peter Pan, down back streets, jumping across the alleyways in a single bound, pretending to fly.

I walked imaginary rooftops, keeping my balance, even though it was just the curb of the sidewalk. Any fall off the curb would be accompanied with a long scream all the way down from the pretended height. Back alleys became the streets of London. Jimmy would play the Artful Dodger, and Al was Fagin. Al's backyard was often the lazy banks of the Mississippi River. He and I would be Tom and Huck. We went around the world and across the nation without leaving West Philly.

I don't know if Al, Jimmy, and Little Mikey knew just how important they were to me, but they were my family. I loved my sister; she was my only blood relative at that time, but I desperately wanted more family. So together, right in the middle of all the violence and craziness of the ghetto, Al, Jimmy, Little Mikey, and I carved out a parallel world of loyal, caring brothers. We created a wonderful place in which we could be little boys with youthful imaginations. And in that make-believe world, we were innocent for just a little while. Our fears were put aside. We were free.

CHAPTER THREE

TORN BETWEEN REALITY AND POSSIBILITY

In the early 60s, my sister and I were blessed to move from the inner city to a place called Darby just outside of Philadelphia. After too many foster homes to count and a succession of disastrous foster parents, this was our final move. I would not see Al, Jimmy, or Little Mikey again. I realized that as much as I wanted friends and family in them, it was out of my control. The reality was that I continually lost people I cared about.

My new foster parents were blue-collar workers who owned their home. For the first time in our lives, my sister and I had comfortable beds with clean sheets that smelled like a fresh spring morning. There were white linen curtains in the windows that swayed in the summer breeze. This home was warm in the winter and cool in the summer. At first, I thought we had landed in a TV dream home! At any moment, the Beaver from *Leave It to Beaver* would stick his head in my room and say, "Hey Wally, want to go out and play?"

Although we never had steak, we ate regular, hearty meals. I wasn't hungry anymore! However, my *Leave It to Beaver* picture shattered at the first violent beating and ruthless reminder that I was not their kid either. I consoled myself that this foster home was light-years better than what we had before, and I accepted that I probably deserved to be beaten. After all, I was ugly, rotten, and undeserving of love.

Even with the beatings, I stubbornly pursued my quest to be a normal and well-balanced *Brady Bunch* kid. My sister and I had seen kids with loving parents, and we tried to believe we could live that way, too, despite our reality.

MULBERRY STREET MARAUDERS

Even though it was a step up from Philly, times were still hard. Christmas of 1962, I looked around at my friends from two-parent families. They found a fancy racer bicycle under their Christmas trees. My foster brother Billy and I received $2 in a small manila envelope and two pairs of knee-high tube socks from the Bargain Basement store. I'll never forget our disappointment—or our solution.

The following spring, our plan went into action one early Saturday morning. Billy and I got up and quietly tiptoed out the back door. The neighborhood was asleep, and it was still dark outside. We made our way to the junkyard and went around to the back, where no one could see us. We stood and contemplated the daunting chain-link fence in front of us. We knew there was a mean old junkyard dog somewhere in there, but that did not deter us. As quietly as possible, we threw a blanket over the barbed wire at the top and successfully scaled the fence.

Once in the junkyard, we went right to our target: a heap of old bicycle parts. We picked out frames and wheels and all the parts we would need. Trip after trip, arms full, we threw our stolen treasure over the fence. We were going back to find a pedal when we awakened the mean old junkyard dog. He ran toward us with the most vicious bark we had ever heard. Our hearts pounded in our chests. I yelled, "Grab that pedal! Let's get out of here!" Fear made us run faster than we'd ever run before.

I didn't leave until Billy had the pedal, and we hit the fence at the same time. The dog was fast on our heels; I was over first, my shirt ripping on the barbed wire. The dog nipped Billy right on the butt, which rocketed him over the fence so fast, he barely seemed to touch the fence at all! On the other side of the fence, we looked at each other, panting for breath. Then we started laughing so hard we could barely move. Billy laughed at my ripped shirt. "You're in trouble."

I laughed at his nipped butt. "You were almost junkyard dog breakfast." Then we decided to get out of there before we woke up the whole neighborhood. I don't remember if I got a beating for the ripped shirt. All I remember is building those bikes in the back alley. We raced the rich kids with their fancy racers, and out of sheer willpower, most of the time, our mixed-matched junkyard racers won. We also won the respect of the rest of the guys on the block. We rode in a group that got larger as time went on. Billy and I had a great story, and I had made new friends. I suspected some of the rich kids wanted a junkyard adventure too.

One day, while watching our old black-and-white TV, a movie came on that captured my imagination. Based on a true story during World War II, it was about a United States Army long-range penetration, special operations, jungle warfare unit called Merrill's Marauders. I loved it so much! The next time I met up with the guys, I told them about the movie. After we were all worked up, I suggested we should be known as the Mulberry Street Marauders. Our new name unanimously approved, we were ready for our first long-range mission: a bike ride adventure.

Our mission (if we chose to accept it) was "to go somewhere we had never gone before," to see things we had never seen before outside of our neighborhood. We planned the trip to be just for a while so we could get back safely without our parents knowing about it. At least, that was the plan.

It was 1963, and as African Americans, we were only allowed to live in the section of Darby called "The Hill." Some of our white neighbors called it "Chicken Hill." We just called it The Hill. Segregation was at its height, and it was enforced. The Hill was surrounded by white neighborhoods, where blacks were not allowed, with the exception of the Darby-Colwyn Junior High School and Darby-Colwyn High School. The school district was integrated. Although Darby was still segregated in housing, the black kids were able to travel to and from school with no problems.

One day, a ragtag group of twelve to fourteen-year-old boys mounted their bikes and headed out to go farther than they had ever been before. There were seven or eight of us, and we raced after each other down undiscovered streets. We would never have gotten permission from our parents/foster parents to go this far, so we just did it. It seemed far to us, but it was just the next neighborhood over.

We spotted a water fountain in Yeadon's Bell Avenue Schoolyard. That fountain looked very inviting to a bunch of thirsty boys. "I'll race you," I yelled to Billy, and we tore off to get to the fountain first. Billy won the race, and he took his reward with a big smile. He bent toward the fountain and slurped the cool water when I heard loud noises behind me. I turned and saw people running out of the houses around us. The men were armed with hammers and wrenches, shaking their fists, and the women were swinging rolling pins. They were all screaming at the top of their lungs, "Get those niggers!"

I poked Billy in the side and yelled at our group to get out of there. We quickly mounted our bikes and rode away as fast as we could, our hearts pounding and fear propelling our young legs. As we rode, more adults came from their homes yelling in a murderous rage, "Get those niggers! How dare you drink out of our fountain!" I don't know why, but I ended up in the rear of our group. I suspect I wanted to make sure everyone got out safely. After all, it was my idea to go for the ride.

A man about thirty years old was right on my tail, waving a wrench over his head. He was just a lunge or two from hitting me. I don't know if I was overconfident or just full of Mulberry Street Marauders' adrenaline, but I looked back into his crazed face and taunted him, "you'll never catch me!" Then I pedaled faster.

After we were safely back to The Hill, we sat and boasted that we weren't scared at all! We were the masters of the narrow escape, and so skilled on our bikes. Those guys never stood a chance of catching us! After all, we were the mighty Mulberry Street Marauders. We would always be victorious!

Martin Luther King, Jr.

Racism raged on, the Mulberry Street Marauders continued, and I discovered a wonderful freedom fighter. That freedom fighter wasn't a buff, suave man. Mrs. Smiley was a middle-aged woman. She had a fire in her belly, the wisdom of Solomon, believed that all people should be free and equal—and recruited some of the Mulberry Street boys to help the cause. Our foster parents gladly volunteered us.

I didn't know what to expect, but we began meeting at her house. The meetings always included adults, young adults, and kids like me. At first, we packed into Mrs. Smiley's living room, but we had to move to the church as the numbers grew. Eager to help, I always followed directions and was willing to set up chairs and clean up afterward. It wasn't long before I rose through the ranks to become vice president of the Junior N.A.A.C.P. in our branch. The next thing I knew, I was walking picket lines and hearing stories of this guy called Martin Luther King, Jr. Even though I had never heard of him, I believed all that was told to me by our leaders.

At the ripe old age of twelve, I had enough of violence for two lifetimes, so the thought of nonviolent protest appealed to me. We sat in restaurants that refused service to colored people. We picketed places of employment that refused to hire colored people. We were treated with fierce contempt. Big, burly white men walked up to us and ripped our picket signs out of our hands. We were shoved, punched, kicked, and spat on. But our fearless leader would be right there, telling us, "Do not repay evil for evil."

For me, 1963 was a confusing time. Picket-sign marches and sit-in protests were common. A couple of times, Mrs. Smiley had to say, "Sit back down, Charles." I couldn't stand to see a man push a woman, and I wanted to fight, but the look in her eyes always calmed my heart. She was a powerful woman and a real civil rights leader. She decided we would go to hear Dr. King speak in Washington, D.C. The next thing I knew, we were all on the bus headed to the nation's capital.

We arrived the day before the historical event. We had no idea how many people would be there. It was August, and the weather couldn't have been more perfect. I had never been to D.C. before. The city seemed enormous, and when we got to the Lincoln Memorial, I could hardly breathe. I was so excited. We came with a busload and cars, maybe thirty or forty of us, but we were a small drop in the sea of faces. I was going to see the man I had heard so much about—hear his voice and see his face. Being there was beyond my wildest dreams.

I had grown a deep loyalty to Martin Luther King, Jr. and the people in his Southern Christian Leadership Conference. I was blessed to attend what we now know as "The March on Washington." I heard his famous "I Have a Dream" speech. But, unfortunately, where I was standing, it was hard to hear clearly. Then he hesitated. I'm told he went off-script when Mahalia Jackson shouted to him, "Tell them about the dream, Martin! Tell them about the dream!"

At that moment, I heard him clearer than ever. It was like no one was there but him and me. He spoke what was in my heart. "I have a dream!" And for the first time in my life, I believed in hope. Right then and there, I, too, had a dream. Sure, I was borrowing his, but it seemed like my dream all the same. I'll never forget that day. It was as if a light switch was flipped in my head. I could be who I was supposed to be. I could be a good person with a gentle spirit. I could also, for the first time, have white friends.

It was a long, strange trip back home. At first, the bus was filled with electricity, everyone buzzing about what had just happened, what we had heard, and how Martin Luther King, Jr.'s words made us feel. I will never forget that energy. It felt like it could light up the city. But as we approached home, the bus grew quiet as we faced the reality of our lives there. How could we, a small group, many of us kids, carry and fulfill this dream?

Nicky

Here was my dilemma: Until now, all of my heroes had been white, and most of them were fictional characters. Many were my heroes, but my new hero was Martin Luther King, Jr., a real man, and a real *black* man. I also had made some white friends. Now, my participation in the civil rights movement put me against many white people, and I *didn't like them.*

When we picketed places for unfair practices against black people, white faces would spit on me, punch me, and shove me. White faces kicked me during a peaceful sit-in protest. One angry white man, who snatched my picket sign out of my hands and pushed me, looked a lot like Hoss Cartwright. Although I know it wasn't Hoss, I didn't know what to think. I would have liked him to act a little more like Hoss because he was scaring me something awful! Hoss was a good guy, but this guy wanted to kill a thirteen-year-old kid.

Could I be both black and human? I wanted to be a good person with a gentle spirit. I also wanted to have black friends and white friends. I protested segregation on the weekends, and I would hang out with my best friend Nicky during the week. I had met him at school, and he was white. He and I became inseparable. Back then, when you saw one of us, you would see the other. Nicky was instrumental in helping me focus on my schoolwork, and we were determined to bring up my grades. We would have great talks about math and English and literature. That year, a teacher said to me, "Charles, you write very well. You could be a writer one day." To this day, whenever I'm writing cursive, I still hold my pen in the unique way he held his.

We were also friends with a kid named Sean. Nicky was Italian, and Sean was Irish. We were all good friends, but it was Nicky who invited me over to his house. I had never been in a white kid's house before, and I didn't know what to expect. I remembered being chased out of the white neighborhood with the fountain, and the people who chased me had looked like they wanted to tear me to pieces. Only because I loved Nicky like a brother did I find the courage to make the scary trip into his white, unfriendly neighborhood where I had been told I didn't belong.

I was rewarded for my courage. Nicky's mom immediately made me feel welcome. She broke out a batch of freshly baked Italian cookies and put them in front of us. Unguarded cookies? That had never happened to me before. I loved them instantly. It wasn't until later that I realized I probably ate way too many! She probably thought I was starved and let me eat as many as I could. In fact, she seemed to delight in my enthusiasm for her cooking.

White kids used to tease Nicky for being my friend, and black kids would tease me for being Nicky's. One day after gym, we were dressing after showers, and Nicky noticed my Murray's hair pomade. I took pride in the waves in my hair back then. I smoothed my hair with the greasy product. Nicky asked if he could try it, and I told him to help himself. Neither one of us thought about how heavy it would be on white people's hair.

Nevertheless, we thought it looked good on him. All slickered up, we admired our hair in the mirror, clueless about what was about to happen. When we got to class, several of the white kids started laughing at Nicky's slicked-down hair. I don't know how Nicky felt, but I was angry. Later, we laughed about the whole thing and agreed it might be a bad idea for him to use Murray's again.

In the early 60s, racial unrest was everywhere. Although Darby-Colwyn's white and black students seemed okay with their particular form of segregation, one hot summer, riots broke out. Most of the Mulberry Street boys did not participate in the looting and fighting, but I couldn't escape the chaos.

Nicky was on his way somewhere near the junior high school when a group of black teenage boys appeared from around the corner. They started with, "Hey white boy, we're going to kick your ..." just when I turned the corner and realized what was happening. I positioned myself between my friend and his attackers.

"What you boys up to?" I asked knowingly, with half a smile just to show confidence. It was the same slight smile my cowboy heroes had right before the showdown.

"We're going to kick this honky's . . . " they replied.

"Not while I'm alive. You'll have to come through me if you want to get to him. He's my friend, and if you ever touch him, I'll hunt you down one by one until I get you all." I put on my best mad-dog look.

The leader said, "You crazy, boy."

"Yeah, and don't forget that," I responded. As fast as it started, it was over, and Nicky never had a problem with those guys again. He went on to have a brilliant career and a great life. I love him and the wonderful memories of him to this day. For a time, his friendship gave me the hope that I might be able to be black and human.

CHAPTER FOUR
1968

In high school, I played one season of football as a third-string, not-very-spectacular quarterback. I also ran pretty well for our track team and turned out to be a fair gymnast. I had no male role model to push me in sports, and all the kids from big families with involved parents had the top spots on the teams. But with Nicky and Sean's help, I made the honor roll and did well until midway through twelfth grade. I was then dropped from college prep class and placed in Bookkeeping for reasons I didn't understand until later.

Circumstances were coming to a head, and I feared they would utterly crush me. I was on the brink of aging out of the foster care system without a parachute. It was a new fear that felt oddly familiar. It screamed, "You're on your own, kid!" The year 1968 was a turning point in my life. The backdrop was the much-hated war in Vietnam and a spirit of rebellion among American young people. Reeling from all this, nobody paid attention to the fact that my little world was falling apart.

I felt like a character in the cartoons I watched, with a heavy anvil of doom hanging over my head. Within months I would be on the streets, by myself in the world. I tried to escape the reality that I was soon to be on my own. Instead, I dove into the fictional lives of the television stars of *Star Trek*, *The Mod Squad*, *Laugh-In*, and *Bewitched*. But the historical events of 1968 also played out on TV screens across the country, bringing them home in a way never possible before. There was no humor or security there.

THE BEAUTY MOVES TO TOWN

The first time I saw Jane, she stood out like a jewel. She was light-complexioned, which was unusual for a black person back then, and all the guys wanted to be in her company. She was smart as a whip, and biology was her favorite subject. She was more advanced than our school curriculum. She also was not prejudiced toward my white friends, like some of our black friends at the time. I loved everything about her, but I knew I did not stand a chance against all the jocks vying for her attention. Still, she was my first love.

Lucky for me, two things drew us together: Jane had a thirst for adventure, and she was a bit of a tomboy. She outshone many of the guys in running and jumping. I guess she noticed me because I thirsted for unconventional adventure as well. Our imaginations synced. We spent hours hunting bugs for her collection. Then we would spend more hours in her garage mounting the bugs. I was crazy about her, and every so often, we would steal a kiss at the end of a summer evening.

There were elements of danger about our relationship. I had to strive to get over my terrible insecurities. But as much as I tried, my low emotional intelligence led me to make some of the worst mistakes. For example, when a guy made advances toward Jane, I got into an argument with him. I found out later she had no interest in him, and she was not happy about the way I had confronted him. She was very independent, which I both loved and feared. We also had to keep our relationship secret because Jane's parents thought I was not good enough for their daughter. In a different world I might have been, but Jane was going to college, and I was destined for the factory or the military. It was the deal-breaker that would break my heart to the core.

My head was filled with the conflicting notions of a senior in high school. I was emotionally immature and had no plan for the future. No one took the time to guide or coach me. My foster parents only told me they were advised by my school principal that I was not college material. This was devastating to hear, as I had worked hard to get good grades.

Other kids were preparing for college, but there were very few blacks in the college prep classes. I had zero support from home. My foster father had a fifth-grade education, and my foster mother had an eighth-grade education. What could they teach a senior in high school? Out of all the foster kids in that household, I was the only one who graduated high school.

I had my friend Nicky and Mr. Laird, my literature teacher, to thank for at least being able to graduate high school, but I had no idea how to get into college, nor was I financially able to do so. I wanted to become a lawyer, but that dream seemed way out of reach. My only hope was the military, but I had no desire to kill anyone or become just another anonymous casualty of the Vietnam War. I was trying to process all this in my immature mind.

My First Drink

On April 3, 1968, Martin Luther King, Jr. told striking black workers in Memphis, Tennessee, "The nation is sick. Trouble is in the land." A racist gunman shot and killed him the next day. On April 4, we were called to a school assembly and told what had happened. It felt as though the bullet that killed MLK had killed me as well. I remember uttering my old curse and new mantra, "They will never let me be anything." I had no idea who "they" were, but that day utterly broke me. The weight of MLK's murder seemed to be the final straw. My life would be hell from then on.

One day soon after, someone brought in a bottle of vodka to a graduation rehearsal. It didn't take long for the word to reach me, "Booze in recreation field after practice." Usually, I would have avoided that, but I decided to go and drink my fill. That day, I had my first drink of booze and my first cigarette. I drank like a real drunk. It seemed like I couldn't get enough of the stuff. The burn of the alcohol going down was comforting, and the effect helped me not to be me for a little while. It allowed me to escape my reality and pain. It washed away my "foster kid" identity, and for a little while, I was strong, courageous, and fully capable of being liked. After that day, I was drunk as often as I could afford it, desperately trying to maintain that amazing feeling.

After graduation, I hung around the Darby area for a while. I rented a room above a dry cleaner on The Hill. Where else could I go? Instead of hanging around Nicky and Sean, my academic friends, I now hung out with people who drank and howled at the moon. I had this newfound freedom from the routines of the foster home: no school, no purpose, just hard work and booze rewards.

THE FREEDOM HOUSE

Remember Mrs. Smiley? That amazing woman went on to bridge the racial divide by opening what was appropriately named the Freedom House. This wonderful house was right on the border of the white neighborhood and black neighborhood. The hope was to serve multiethnic needs. No one would be denied help. It was a good endeavor, and I supported it as much as I could. I wasn't that good kid anymore, but I still had goodness in me, I guess. I held onto my morals, and a voice of reason was still echoing faintly in the back of my head. Nevertheless, I was quickly turning into a wine-drinking, pot-smoking hippie.

One of my white hippie friends told me of a nefarious plot to burn down the Freedom House. A militant group of young white guys about our age had bottles of gasoline to set it ablaze. So I gathered my old friends, the Mulberry Street Marauders, and we planned our intervention. Perhaps this would be our last hurrah as a team, and we would go out in a blaze of glory, like heroes.

My plan was that we would use the Robin Hood strategy in combination with a semi-nonviolent surprise. Not everybody agreed with the nonviolent part of the plan, but in the end, we all agreed that out of respect for Mrs. Smiley, it would be best.

Our intel was good. We found out that the leader of the white guys lived on the hill above the Freedom House. The enemy would rally there and come down a path through the woods to the rear of the house.

That evening, just around dusk, we surrounded the path behind the house at a strategic chokepoint. Cleverly, many of us hid in the tree branches overhead. Some of us, especially the bigger guys, hid in the thick bushes next to the path. As darkness approached, we had to shush each other several times when one or two of us would giggle. It was pitch black when we heard voices approaching. The gang of young men was so proud of their scheme. We could overhear them bragging about that "expletive" house burning to the ground.

We remained silent; I was in a tree as they walked directly under me. Then, just when they got to the point of no escape, I yelled, "Now!" We screamed wildly, dropping out of trees and jumping out of bushes.

One white guy cried out, "The niggers are dropping out of trees. They've got me! Help!"

Another yelled, "Run!"

There was so much screaming and yelling, they dropped their bottles of gasoline and ran through the woods yelling, "Those niggers are crazy! They got Bob! Let's get out of here!"

As quick as it started, it was over. After some verbal thrashing and threats to turn them over to the cops, we let Bob and the others we had caught go. I kept hearing Mrs. Smiley's teachings in my head. "We do not use violence. We do not throw punches. We do no physical harm to another person, no matter what." I don't remember anyone throwing a single punch. I think the surprise was enough to scare them, and The Freedom House was never threatened again. It went on just as Mrs. Smiley planned, to do good for all people.

CHAPTER FIVE
HIGHS AND LOWS

My life was going nowhere fast. Living alone in that dank room above the dry cleaners was depressing, and drinking was my escape. I decided to join the Navy. It was the slogan that got me: "Join the Navy and see the world." I joined, and it wasn't long before I was assigned to be a squad leader. Unfortunately, as shore patrol and CID guard, I saw little more than the Great Lakes, Chicago, and San Diego. That was nice, but not really "the world."

After so many months in the Navy, I dropped acid and smoked weed. I bought the drugs from a fourteen-year-old Mexican kid I had met at the cheap cinema in San Diego. He wanted me to describe the town where I lived back east as if he had dreams to go somewhere else. It seemed he, too, was looking for a different reality. He didn't smoke; he just hung around the movies and sold the stuff to people. I guess he liked talking to me. Maybe I wasn't as scary as some of his other customers. I didn't get it then, but he had to be working for a gang. Again, the gangs often use minors to sell for them, because minors receive lighter sentences if caught.

One day, a returning Vietnam vet introduced me to China-white heroin. This drug took me so far outside of myself, I decided right then I wanted to be in that place of oblivion forever. I didn't have to feel so alone. Finally, I could count on something to make me feel nothing. Unfortunately, it also made me reckless.

I loved the Navy, but the price of addiction is high. One day I was hanging over the side of the U.S Canberra, a massive Baltimore Class heavy cruiser. I was high above the ocean, cleaning the fog lights and scraping old paint flakes off the bow. A sailor who had been taunting me for being black stood over the rope that suspended me and began to stroke his knife across the rope, saying, "Your body won't wash up for a while. It doesn't matter how well you can swim, boy. The impact will kill you. This is how we make niggers disappear, boy."

I wasted no time climbing up that rope faster than Tarzan. The sailor kept trying to cut the rope, but I grabbed the rail and swung over before he could. You know the look people have when their plans have gone wrong? That's the look I saw in his eyes. He couldn't believe I was standing right in front of him. He grabbed me by the collar and called me a nigger again, which is when I forgot Mrs. Smiley's advice. I hauled off and punched him in the mouth.

Other sailors had to pull me off him, so it did not look good for me. I washed out of the Navy, like everything else I had ever wanted. Any career I would have had by leaving in good standing was gone. It's one of my deepest regrets. To this day, I love military heroes and wish I could have been one.

RETURN TO PHILLY

I left California and returned to Pennsylvania because I knew Jane was there. I could not stop loving her, and we got back together. I also joined a hippie community and convinced her to hang out with us. I had found my place in the world, or so I thought. I used acid, downers, booze, and a little heroin at first. Eventually, I did heroin as much as I could afford. Since I was living in the commune, my whole paycheck was used to stay high.

I managed to keep a manual labor job, lifting 100-pound bags of flour and sugar and stacking them on pallets and trucks. I also worked in a paint factory, mixing solvents and pigments. In the paint factory, workers found amusement by having conversations with Alvin, the oldest worker in the plant. They mocked him, asking simple questions to see how long it took his brain to process an answer. Even when asked, "What's your name?" he would pause for a couple of seconds to answer. We would leave work at the end of the day, but the solvent in our lungs would not quickly leave us. I didn't laugh at Alvin because I knew the solvent was slowly turning all of us into him.

I left the paint factory job and started driving trucks for a company. My life was draining away, slipping through my fingers, and I didn't care. Every weekend with Jane was an adventure. I was committed to being a peace-loving hippie. I listened to music like: "All Along the Watchtower," by Hendrix; "Suzi Q," by C.C.R.; "Going Up the Country," by Canned Heat; "Mighty Quinn," by Manfred Mann; "Tighten Up," by Archie Bell; and "I Wish It Would Rain," by the Temptations.

I grew my hair into a rich Afro and hung out with the fringe, hippie, peace-loving communities. I went to concerts, smoked weed, and dropped acid. Since I could do more dope than anyone else most of the time, I was a hit. It seemed as if I had star power, but in truth, I was burning out fast. I was daring and edgy because the drugs were in control. I would risk my whole life for a thrill and approval.

I worked hard at my job because it supported my drug habit. The only time I was sober was when I was driving that big truck. I drove well, and the company loved my work. I thought I concealed my drug use successfully, although I was probably delusional. Everybody knew I was loaded. This is the part of addiction that tightens the noose and closes off all escape routes, like a Venus flytrap. I didn't know it, but I was deep in the sticky trap of addiction, and my life was slipping away.

For a while, I tried to remain sober for Jane. Instead, I became instrumental in getting her involved with drugs. My drinking increased, and one day we dropped acid and went to the shore. It was so wonderful there; we lost track of time. We got back late, and Jane's parents were furious. Jane lied and said she had been with girlfriends. Her parents believed her.

Encouraged by the events of the day, I decided I would take my chances to win Jane's heart for good. In my mind, I knew what I had to do. The next day, I went to Jane's mom and confessed fully about the night before. I then asked for Jane's hand in marriage. After all, I had to marry this wonderful girl! My delusional plan didn't quite work out. Jane's mom immediately banned me from seeing her again. I understood and didn't argue. Jane was on her way to college to become a doctor, and I was washed out of the military and on my way to nowhere. I had accumulated failure after failure, and I was a big fat zero once again. Everybody was right about me.

I experienced terrible grief. My gut heaved from crying until I threw up. Finally, a gut punch that made me puke, but it wasn't from a guy. This went on for days. Finally, I bought a huge batch of sleeping pills from one of my suppliers and took them all. This would be my first suicide attempt. My addict friends took my dying body to the clubhouse of a motorcycle gang. We often hung out with them, and they were the number-one source for acid and meth. They decided to shoot me up with meth in an attempt to revive me. After shooting me up with a couple of massive doses of meth, they dumped my body in front of Fitzgerald Mercy Hospital and drove off.

Although I was unconscious in the ICU, I was aware of my spirit floating next to the ceiling. I looked down on my lifeless body, the doctors and nurses scrambling around me, inserting tubes and needles to try to bring me back to life. Then, after floating for a while, a voice that wasn't loud but seemed to be everywhere said, "Go back."

I woke up, and soon I was discharged from the hospital. I called my friends to pick me up. When they did, I asked, "What happened yesterday?"

They said, "Yesterday? It's been three days, buddy! Three days ago, we dropped you off at the hospital. You were dead."

Jane's rejection and my encounter with death left me even more emotionally and spiritually crushed. I felt like a zombie, even when I wasn't drinking and on drugs. This was not my dream. I was the kid who dreamed of being like Matt Dillon of Dodge City or Martin Luther King, Jr. I was the kid who was the leader of the Mulberry Marauders and the Junior NAACP. I never dreamed I would become a hopeless addict.

THE LITTLE OLD LADY

Some friends who cared for me (I don't know why they cared) finally got me into rehab in Norristown, Pennsylvania. I did poorly there, getting in with other addicts who didn't want recovery any more than I did. Eventually, the management kicked me out of the inpatient program and referred me to the outpatient program in town. Outside of the treatment center, the temptation was too much. I started dealing dope for a Black Muslim sect that controlled most of the heroin trade in North Philly. They were expanding to smaller towns like Norristown, and they were a ruthless bunch.

This group killed people to take over drug territory—just to establish their reputation as murderous. You did not want to mess with them! One ambitious member decided to trust me with a bunch of dope to sell for him. Almost immediately, I was my own best customer. I did all the dope myself, and when he came back a couple of days later to collect his money, I hid. They had just killed a friend of mine. They also killed a guy who would not deal for them and chopped up his body. They left his head on his doorstep to send a brutal message to all who would oppose them. Now they were hunting me.

I locked myself in this old house, barricading the doors. I would only sneak out at night. My friend Phil brought me food and drugs when he could. Then, one day, there was a knock on the front door. "Who is it?" I asked.

"It's me, Phil," my friend answered. I opened the door just a crack. Phil's eyes told the whole story. I tried to push the door shut, but it was kicked in by a huge, angry man. He grabbed me by the neck and started dragging me to the back of the house. "You're a dead man!" he yelled.

I started talking as fast as I could. "I'll make your money back! I promise! Please, don't kill me!"

After pounding on me, half out of breath, he stopped suddenly and said, "I don't know why I don't just kill you now. Have my money by Friday, and I'll let you live. There are no more chances for you, punk, and if you try to run, my people will find you with a green light (shoot-on-sight order) on your head." His whole hand covered my face as he pushed me down one last time, and then he left.

I had no idea how I was going to make their money back, and, to complicate matters, I was dope-sick and scared. I had a replica gun that I carried occasionally in my dangerous neighborhood. It was authentic looking, and I had used it to get out of a couple of tricky situations. It's a miracle I didn't get shot for having it. It was getting late, and I couldn't figure out what to do. As I was walking by a store, for some strange reason, I thought it would be a good idea to go in, pull out my fake gun, and rob it.

I walked in, pretending to look around. There were no other customers in the store and only a little old lady behind the counter. I walked up, and she asked, "Can I help you, young man?"

I answered in the most threatening voice I could muster, "Give me all the money in the register, old lady, and there won't be any trouble. Do it quickly!"

Unimpressed, the gray-haired lady looked me right in the eyes and said, "Young man, I know you're troubled, but you don't have to worry; God will take care of you."

Now I was in a panic. I needed to get the money for the Muslim dealers, so I doubled down on my threats. "If you don't open that register and give me that money, I'm going to start shooting." I waved the gun frantically.

The old lady kept saying, "I'm not worried or afraid. The Holy Spirit is here, and He is going to protect us both." Then, looking me in the eyes, she said again very slowly, "God will take care of you."

I was not sure what to say at this point. Finally, I decided to give up. I said, "You're crazy, old lady," put my fake gun back into my belt, and walked out.

The next day, in my outpatient program, my counselor asked, "Charles, what were you doing in that Bible store last night? I got so excited that you had found God; I started to stop and get out of my car to talk to you."

I was stunned. Had I tried to rob a *Bible store*? "Oh, I don't know. I think I was looking for a good Bible," I lied.

"Did you find one?" he asked.

"I haven't made up my mind yet," I replied as I walked away. How far I had fallen! I would never harm a woman, especially a little old lady. I didn't practice any faith and didn't know the Bible, but I had a fear of God. Now I was doing all the things I thought I'd never do.

I still did not have the money I owed the Muslims. I headed home resigned to be a dead man. Sure enough, a man stepped out of a car and walked toward me. He could have killed me right then and there, and no one in the neighborhood would have cared. He said, "I don't know why I'm doing this, but take this dope and make up the money. Give it all to me by Friday, and your debt is paid."

I stood for a few minutes in a daze. These Muslims didn't do this. I was given a second chance by a stone-cold killer. Even though I was dope-sick, I dared not mess up this time. I didn't care about profit. I made his money, and I paid my debt. That next week, a guy named Bill gave me a job doing drywall and a place to live out of that neighborhood. I felt lucky—like I was the master of the narrow escape. But I was haunted by these questions: Had the little old lady in the Bible store been right? Had God protected both of us? Had He taken care of me?

Did I stop using? No. All my paychecks still went to dope. I didn't get better, but I did get more careful—or so I thought.

CHAPTER SIX
INTO OBLIVION

I felt like a pinball in a machine that some evil wizard was playing, bouncing me from calamity to calamity, year after year, decade after decade. I lived in the most confusing, depressing, and scary world a man could experience. I saw a young man shot and killed over one dollar during a drug buy, but I kept buying. Heroin felt like the best solution for the pain and chaos in my life. When wasted in oblivion, the pain seemed to lessen, and the clamor of chaos subsided for a little while. But both the pain and the chaos always came back with a vengeance. It seemed like heroin would say to me, "You've got to do anything to get to me," day after day, week after week.

I learned every trick in the book to manage my addiction, but there was one I had not learned—abstinence. I had a good work ethic and cleaned up pretty well. I found a decent job and even married a sweet young lady who gave me my one and only son. We lived in Philadelphia on the 21st floor of an amazing high-rise. I was working in maintenance at a hospital, and on the side, I was moving pounds of weed for a big boss. The lifestyle got to be too much for my wife, so she left my son and me. I tried to raise my boy while addicted, doing the best I could for ten years. My son Carlos and I had great times, especially when I was high. I would treat him to anything and play in the park with him as if I was a kid, too. I could be his best bud, but I failed at being his dad.

I got into a bar fight in South Philly on my lunch break one day. I messed the guy up pretty bad and then went back to work as if nothing happened. Two huge cops showed up at my job to arrest me. I couldn't afford the high-rise after I lost my job, so I moved back to Darby. Rent was cheaper, so things were a little better. I kept Carlos clean for school and well-fed, but I had very little else to offer him. Unless I was high, I did not talk to him. We would just sit in silence.

One day I was so dope-sick, I knew I couldn't go on taking care of Carlos anymore. I looked at him, and he looked back with big, sad eyes. That look was too much for me to bear. I packed his clothes and took him to his mother. After that, things quickly spiraled out of control. I lost all hope.

I ended up in Chester, Pennsylvania, a small city not far from Philadelphia. I was beaten up pretty badly. I had very few teeth left in my mouth, and I was dirty and unkempt from living in any abandoned building I could find. I worked hard driving a truck, loading and unloading boxcars of thousands of pounds of flour and sugar. I spent all my earnings on drugs and ate at a local Christian mission. At night, when I was alone, I cried out in desperation, "Why, why do I always lose? Why am I so unlovable? How did I end up so ugly and messed up?"

Addicts commit many kinds of crimes to get dope. Some specialize in robberies, usually using guns to catch people by surprise. Some addicts become burglars. Unlike robbers, burglars never want to see people while committing their crimes. They case homes or businesses, and when no one is around, they break in and take as much as they can carry. Other addicts sell drugs. Some deal drugs all day, and that is their source of income. Then, they get their fix at night. Unfortunately, they generally become their own best customer, getting in trouble with their suppliers and ripping off the customers who had come to trust them.

I tried everything, but I was no good at any of these. So, I worked the hardest jobs, the jobs no one else wanted. That was my specialty. I would work myself into exhaustion and take all my earnings to the drug dealer. You'd think that was the safe way to go, but nothing is safe in the world of an addict. When the robbers came to rob me and put guns to my head, I would have rather died than give them my hard-earned drugs. I'd say, "Nope, I ain't got nothing!" It's a miracle I wasn't killed a hundred times over.

Sometimes, the police would come and hassle or arrest me. They almost always went to extremes with violence. They would beat me half to death when they couldn't find drugs. They made up anything to charge me, just to lock me up so they could cover up their brutal tactics. Poor people who looked like me never won in the justice system. Occasionally, I would encounter policemen who would take pity on me, probably because I was a nonviolent criminal, and I always spoke courteously to them: "Yes sir, no sir, I'm sorry, sir." Even when I was lying to them, I was courteous. I don't think they believed my lies, but when they really looked at me, they didn't see a seasoned criminal; they saw a sorry mess.

The life of an addict is filled with death. I can't tell you how many times I had a gun aimed at my head or received death threats. I've been sucker-punched a few times when I wasn't alert or paying attention. I must have a hard head because I've never been knocked out, but I've been hit in the head twice with baseball bats and twice with two-by-fours. I've been stabbed and shot, still holding on to drugs.

ABANDOMINIUM

This isn't a typo or misspelling. I lived in an abandominium, which was an abandoned house. Sometimes I lived with several other colorful characters. Lawnmower Man gained his moniker because he stole a lot of lawnmowers. He lived in my abandominium for a short time. One day, I came downstairs, and Lawnmower Man noticed I had a little pep in my step. A group of people had taken an interest in me, and they encouraged me to get a bridge for my missing teeth. They had given me some money for dental work the day before. They had also arranged for a dentist to do the job at a ridiculously reduced rate. All I had to do was get the money to him this particular morning.

Lawnmower Man asked, "Where you are going this fine morning, all cheery-eyed?" I should never have answered, but I did.

"Some people gave me some money to get my teeth fixed today. I'm getting some new teeth."

Lawnmower Man said, "You've got money?"

"Yeah, and don't get any ideas. I promised to use this money for my teeth."

He said, "You don't need no teeth. You've got that rugged look."

"What are you talking about, Lawnmower Man? I look like a vampire!" All my front teeth were missing except my canines.

"Man, don't you know the ladies love that vampire look. Makes you look dangerous. They love it." It was hard enough doing the right thing with money burning in my pocket. The last thing I needed was a cheering section telling me to do the wrong thing.

I turned around and looked in the broken piece of mirror by the door. I smiled at my reflection and said, "You know what, Lawnmower Man? I do have that rugged look. I ain't half bad."

I don't know what I saw in the mirror that day, because I was malnourished and unkempt. I was a shell of a man with a huge gap in my smile. Nevertheless, the thought of getting high was overwhelming. "I'll tell you what, Lawnmower Man. Today's your lucky day. Let's go get high. My treat."

"Best thing I've heard all day," he said with a smile on his face. There would be no teeth for me, and the money was smoked away. Not long after that day, Lawnmower Man died from some bad dope. It could have just as easily been me.

One day, I left my abandominium to score some drugs. I had walked through this gauntlet of danger many times before. My keen sense of survival was acutely aware that there were many ways to get robbed or murdered in this dangerous neighborhood. I, however, had become numb to all of it. I was like the walking dead. Any thug could see I had very little life left, and the murderers would look at me as an easy body to drop, an easy practice kill for a young, up-and-coming killer. There would be no investigation into who killed me. I was in my late 40s, but I looked 60.

I bought three bags of cocaine, because it had become nearly impossible for me to find a vein to shoot up heroin. I had acquired a crack cocaine habit that was a monster of a slave master, even at the risk of my life. As I returned to my castle, I walked right through the middle of a group of laughing young thugs. Then I realized they were laughing at me. I didn't blame them. I was dirty, unkempt, stinky, and so obviously homeless. Besides, I had the antidote to all ridicule and shame in my pocket. One puff and their laughter and name-calling would vanish into smoke. For a sweet while, I would feel nothing.

My guard was down, and it was only a few strides later that I heard the blast and felt the sting. One of the thugs had shot me in the back of my head. Apparently, they were just shooting for fun, since they were laughing hysterically as I went down. Just before losing consciousness, I heard one of them say, "Look at all that blood. He's leaking like a mother—"

I woke up in the hospital. My head was bandaged in a turban-like fashion, there was a catheter in me, and I was intravenously attached to bags of blood and saline. I started to come back to the very place I did not want to be: consciousness. I felt acutely aware of every single sorrow I had accumulated and carried with me over my lifetime, and they overwhelmed me. It was too much.

I looked at the pile of blood-stained clothing draped over a chair, and for some reason, I just knew the drugs were in my pocket. It was as though they were talking to me, like they had an evil, spiritual connection to me and possessed my soul. What I did next boggles my mind. I gently took the catheter out, and seeing blood shoot through the clear plastic tube did not deter me. I took out the intravenous connection, a process oddly familiar since I had grown comfortable around needles. With my hospital robe to cover me, I put on my bloody military jacket, slipped my hand in my right-hand pocket, and felt the comfort of the three bags of cocaine. Soon, they would be my salvation. Nothing could stop me now.

The little nurse noticed me and charged over, bouncing on her toes and trying to make eye contact. She said, "You can't leave, Mr. Knuckles. You still have a bullet in your head." She said this over and over as she tried to get me back to my bed. But she was no match for the powerful god I clutched in my hand. A doctor joined us and tried to persuade me to stay, but I stood my ground. I signed a release form that I was leaving against medical advice and left.

I walked all the way from the hospital to my abandominium with a bloody turban on my head. I did not give the nurse time to change it, because I was on a mission. Those funky old shoes could not get me home fast enough. As soon as I walked through the doorway of my room, the anticipation of getting high almost made my head explode. I thought my stomach was going to flip out of my body. I would soon be in that old familiar place with my old friend "oblivion." Once again, I would feel no pain, have no more worries, and forget the bullet throbbing in my head.

After carefully cooking the cocaine into crack, I lit up and took a deep draw. "Oh yeah, baby. It's going to take me." But it didn't. I thought, *Okay, the next hit is gonna do it.* Still nothing. *After all I've been through, is this some kind of cosmic joke?* I knew this dope was good. I went to the right guy. I did everything right, except for the getting shot part—but even after three bags of primo dope, I could not get high. The only thing I felt was a presence of darkness. An evil voice in my head kept saying- *Those guys were right. You do know that you deserve to die. You're nothing, a zero. Just finish the job and kill yourself. Do it. Do it. You know what you have to do.*

It was the stuff horror movies are made of. It was like I was a robot, obeying the voice of the person programming me. I fashioned a rope to a fixture on the ceiling. I knew it would work, because the guy who had had this room before me hung himself in the very same way. I got up on the only chair in the room, put the rope around my neck, cinched it tight, and stepped off into what I hoped would be the final oblivion.

I don't know what happened next.

I don't have a clue how the rope was removed from my neck. I had been resolute. I had been in the Navy, so I knew how to tie a knot! The knot was true, and I was determined to die. I don't remember walking the city blocks or crossing streets. My only memory is opening the front door of a Christian recovery center and walking in.

When I opened that door, I stepped back into real time.

CHAPTER SEVEN
OUT OF DARKNESS

Some people told me not to include this part, that I might want to tone down the miracle talk, but it is the truth. From the moment I stepped off the chair into oblivion until I arrived at the recovery center, I remember nothing. It was as if Jesus caught me, untied the rope around my neck, and delivered me to the center. It was my miracle.

However, I do vividly remember scaring the crap out of the receptionist when I walked into the center! She took one look at me with my bloody head and moved away. She retreated backwards down the hall, looking like she was seeing a real zombie and saying over and over, "You can't come in here right now. There's nobody here. Everybody's in a meeting. Come back later."

I didn't know what to say, so I just said, "I can't leave, lady. If I leave, I'll die." I knew if I walked out that door, I would be a dead man. Still, the frightened receptionist kept asking me to leave. At that moment, I remembered the many civil rights sit-in protests of my childhood. When we were told to leave, we just sat down; so, I just sat down right there in the front hall! Even in my diminished state of 150 pounds, I knew she probably could not (and would not try to) pick me up and haul me out. She realized this as well, and she became even more frustrated and determined that I should leave.

I was as wide-eyed and frightened as the receptionist when a door down the hall opened, and out walked a tall man. I recognized him as the man who ran the feeding program I frequented. I often noticed him looking my way as I gathered all the food I could. I was very clever at keeping a healthy distance from him, but I had always felt his eyes on me. I was pretty sure I looked like a savage to him, stuffing food in a dirty old margarine tub so I could get back in line for more food. Each time, I tried to act like it was my first time getting served. In my mind, I fooled them every time.

The memory ran through my mind as I sat there. The tall man had watched me but never approached me—until now. He walked right up to me, and I knew he was going to kick me out before I could plead my case. I was sure, after watching me steal all that food, he would grab me by the collar and throw me out the door. To avoid getting sucker punched sitting down, I stood up and braced for the worst—and he *hugged* me!

This was the first human contact I had had in a very long time. He didn't let up, either! He just held me in his arms until my knees began to give way. He totally disarmed me. I let out a sigh, releasing the breath I had been holding. How many years had I been holding that breath? It seemed like I had been holding it forever. Then the tall man leaned in closer and whispered, "We've been waiting for you."

Wait! Waiting for *me?* What did he mean? I was a zero, a loser, a petty thief. I was a liar, a no-good, insignificant, unwanted fly on a horse's behind. These were all the things I had heard most of my life, the names that bounced around in my head as I put that noose around my neck. And now this man was telling me, "We've been waiting for you." If I had been able to cry, I would have liked to have cried.

I can identify this moment as the start of my conscious experience of God's love. The tall man's unexpected welcome was my first glimpse of the face of Christ Jesus.

THE BATHROOM

A few days after I started my rehab program, a staff member lined us up and asked for a volunteer to clean the restrooms. Our homeless guests used these two bathrooms to wash up before the evening meal, so they were unbearably nasty. I had learned from my so-called bros in recovery: never, ever volunteer for anything. Volunteering was assumed to be a sucker's play. Only fools volunteered. But no sooner had the words left the staff member's mouth than my hand went up. I felt like it was the right thing to do. Still, the voice in my head asked, "Are you sure you know what you're doing, boy?" No! Yet, I heard myself say out loud, "Yes, I'll clean the bathrooms."

As my trembling voice broke the silence, everyone looked around to see who the fool was. It seemed like all their heads turned in unison to look at me. Some of the guys snickered, but most just breathed a sigh of relief that it wouldn't have to be them. No one in their right mind wanted to do this nasty job. These bathrooms were used in the evening by 80 to 100 people, most of whom suffered the elements outside all day and some all night. Many did not have a place to wash or go to the bathroom. The men's room had one toilet, one urinal, and one sink, and sometimes their use was interchangeable. You wouldn't want to use the sink to wash your hands, and don't even consider washing your face there.

The lady's room had one toilet and one sink. By the time our homeless guests had finished there, it had looked and smelled like a battle zone. The smell coming from these bathrooms was like a sewage bomb, and everything around them, including the chapel, smelled like ground zero. No one in their right mind wanted anything to do with the cleanup. The job was hazmat-level.

Those living in the recovery center who were assigned to bathroom cleanup would mysteriously disappear, scattering like roaches when the lights were turned on. No resident ever used these bathrooms. And here I was, with my hand up and a goofy expression on my face. For some reason I couldn't understand; I wanted to clean the dirtiest bathrooms imaginable.

What was I thinking? I'm not sure, but I wasn't thinking of bathrooms. For the first time in my life, I was thinking how grateful I was for being rescued. At that point, I couldn't remember being grateful for anything but a bag of drugs and a place to get high. This was a different kind of gratitude. It felt peaceful, empowering, and strange all at the same time. So, I cleaned the bathrooms every day from then on, even on Sundays. Those bathrooms were so clean; the staff would use them instead of the bathrooms designated for them!

Two weeks into my new cleaning regimen, an unexplainable event happened I'll never forget. While cleaning a hard-to-reach area behind the toilet on my hands and knees, I suddenly had a revelation beyond my capacity. I realized that Jesus was spiritually doing to me what I was physically doing to the bathroom. He was cleaning areas in me that were disgusting. He was cleaning those areas I had buried and stowed away because I couldn't bear to look at them. He was cleaning my deep, infected wounds. Jesus was touching the hard-to-reach places deep in my soul. He was restoring my dirty, hard heart to something clean and soft again. He was restoring my soul. As I made the bathroom usable again, Jesus was making me useable. He was giving me value and purpose.

Still on my knees, I looked up and prayed what I'm sure is probably one of the worst prayers ever spoken. "If You would have me, I mean take me into Your crew and all, I'll be whatever You want. I'll be the least of your people. Bottom rung." And just to seal the deal with Him, I said, "If You'll have me, I'll even clean bathrooms in Heaven." When I stood up from that prayer, something happened. I had not changed physically, but I was different inside.

I had smoked for over 30 years. I had been homeless and hopelessly addicted, so I often smoked cigarette butts I found on the ground or in public ashtrays. As I stood up from praying, I noticed a full, unopened pack of cigarettes in my shirt pocket. I had just earned it by helping another resident. I looked down at the pack of cigarettes and heard myself say, "This ain't right," and threw it into a dumpster. I have not smoked since. In just a moment, that quickly, Jesus saved me and delivered me from what is reportedly one of the hardest habits to break.

I was learning that nothing is too hard for God.

DRY BONES NO MORE

When I was still on the streets and came to the mission for food, volunteers from different churches held a short service before the meal. About twice a month, Bill and Chris would come to volunteer. Bill would play his guitar, and he and his wife Chris would lead us in song. Chris would read devotions from *Daily Bread* or other Christian devotional booklets, and we would end with a song and prayer before we would eat. Bill and Chris would then go to the cafeteria and be on the serving line, serving us as if they loved being there. At the time, it was a total mystery to me why they wanted to spend time with us. Back then, I would never have admitted it, but the outright demonstration of their faith touched me deeply.

Now, I know them better. I know it's just who they are in their walk with Jesus. People like them were the best of the center because those of us who were homeless and addicted were also people who had lost hope. Volunteers like Bill and Chris were beacons of hope that brought us joy. The staff was paid to be there eight hours a day, but we loved to see people from different walks of life going out of their way to spend time with us. It was a clear message that said, "You're worth it," when many of us were feeling worthless.

The services were different every time. Sometimes there was music, sing-along favorites with guitar players or a piano player, and the volunteers inspired us as they led us in song. When the spirit really moved us, a grateful recovering addict might share their reason for hope. That show of faith touched me even when I couldn't admit it. I told myself that I was just there for food and would get impatient during the service, yearning for the meal that followed. But my heart was slowly opening to hear the truth of God's Word.

When I was homeless, the food at the mission gave me a little physical strength, which I used to go back out and feed my addiction. Now, I was receiving spiritual food, hearing that the way God thought about me was not how I had always thought about myself, that what He said about me was not what other people had said about me. His plans for my life were a lot different from the world's or anyone else's plans for me. I drank in the services and had a big appetite for spiritual food. Bill and Chris became my friends. Their invitation to the Gospel of Jesus Christ meant, "Come worship with us," and I did.

During one of these pre-meal services, a layman preacher, an ex-addict, explained a passage of Scripture I had recently read: Ezekiel 37:1–14, the story of the valley of dry bones. When he read the part that said, "The hand of the Lord came upon me and brought me out in the Spirit of the Lord, and set me down in the midst of the valley, and it was full of bones," I felt the presence of the Lord. There must have been eighty people there, but I felt like it was just the speaker, Jesus, and me. I was in Delaware Valley, and he was talking about a valley. It was also filled with dry bones all around me, but I wasn't Ezekiel. Instead, I, too, was a pile of dry bones among the other.

The speaker went into the details of how the Lord asked Ezekiel, "Can these bones live?" Then the Lord instructed Ezekiel to say, "O dry bones, hear the word of the Lord! Thus, says the Lord God to these bones: Surely, I will cause breath to enter into you, and you shall live." Right then and there, I asked my first question of the Lord in my new, born-again spirit, "Can these, my dry bones, live?"

For the first time, I heard the Lord answer, "Yes."

Was His voice audible, or did I hear His voice in my heart? My answer was yes to both! He gave me just what I needed. I would go on to make myself available to hear and to believe. Everything would be different now. This was my game-changer! Hearing Him changed the way I lived life. I was no longer alone, and I didn't have to rely on my own strength anymore.

Many missions have stopped the practice of talking about Jesus, reading the Bible and Christian literature, or worshipping in song before serving a meal to the homeless. They stopped to appease government food banks and whatever other assistance the government might give them. If a Christian, nonprofit homeless shelter or recovery center uses government food to feed poor people, you cannot mention or talk about Jesus. Without a doubt, this is a huge mistake and a very bad interpretation of the First Amendment of the Constitution.

A free meal does not give people freedom, but I know from experience that a relationship with Jesus does. When a government hands out food to the poor, then dictates what can and cannot be said during the meal, that is oppression. To use food as leverage against Christianity is not something this country should be proud of, as only Jesus can transform the human heart and mind. He turned me from a rebellious liar and thief into someone who took joy in obeying, serving and helping. Truthfully, I was so grateful to God; I would have done anything anyone in the program asked me to do. I would have climbed on the roof, stood on one foot, rubbed my belly counter-clockwise, and hopped up and down on one foot while patting my head—as long as they liked!

Because of God's love and grace, I experienced little to no discomfort as I detoxed from the hard drugs, and I have told you about the miracle of losing all desire for cigarettes. The same Jesus to whom I prayed that awful prayer kept me in His arms, comforted me, and made my rough road smoother. We all know a guy who is happy and upbeat even in the middle of hard situations. Well, that was me! I probably annoyed some of the other residents and frustrated some staff, but they couldn't deny that I was a walking miracle.

Back then, one method in the recovery process was to humiliate and break the client down, then hopefully build them back up. When staff tried this approach on me, I think I frustrated them a bit. I was already broken, and after my encounter in the bathroom, I looked to Jesus in everything. So, when I was asked to do the most demeaning chore, I relished the opportunity. I would ask things like, "After I clean up the pantry, would you like me to scrub the loading dock too?"

When we were assigned homework, I would finish it that evening, even though it wasn't due until the next week. Then I would work on floors while other guys in the program watched TV. I didn't consider that nobody liked me. In a way, working with a smile on my face was my detox, and it drove some people crazy. I didn't care, because my old dry bones were now full of a life I had never imagined possible.

BECOMING THE MAN I
WAS SUPPOSED TO BE

Less than a year into the program, I started teaching my fellow recovering alcoholics and addicts about gratitude and obedience. Literally, I was teaching the Relapse Prevention course! It was stuff I had learned from the shelter manager. He was the only clinically trained staff member. Thanks to him, I knew Relapse Prevention like the back of my hand, so he let me facilitate classes. I researched and learned the biblical principles for a complete recovery. For those desperate to be totally free, like myself, gratitude to God and obedience to the authorities He placed over us are two of the most critical elements in our recovery. Joy comes naturally as we recover and seek a life with Jesus. Once the Holy Spirit revealed this truth to me, I had to share it, and I was telling everyone.

Even though my outlook on life was more positive, life in the Christian recovery center wasn't easy. God kept teaching me, and I had a steep learning curve. Not unlike Mowgli, the boy raised by wolves in *The Jungle Book*, I had been a savage. I had to relearn just about everything all over again and unlearn other things, but I was eager to do just that.

The staff consisted of kind and well-meaning people, but I don't think anyone was trained to deal with our kinds of problems. One staff member was an overweight church elder who spouted archaic clichés like, "Just say no," or "Keep it simple, stupid." The other was a blind lady who was pursuing her pastoral ordination. Some men who still had addicted minds would routinely take advantage of her inability to see them, do bad things, and later laugh about their antics. The director of the program had just been fired for stealing donations. There was one staff member who understood recovery, but he had very little influence over the staff who were not trained. Things were a mess, and I think the staff was also afraid of some of the residents. Often, I was on my own.

Then a "southern gentleman" who embodied the name arrived. He had come from Arkansas to turn things around. He was kind and gentle, but also brave and strong. He modeled the image of masculinity that men like me needed to see. One day, he said to me, "Charles Knuckles, you're the real deal." I knew how to put one foot in front of the other, but I didn't know how to believe in myself. This was different than what I heard from the other staff members. The gentleman from Arkansas picked up on that and did everything he could do to build me up.

One day I was in the cafeteria, and a resident from a hardcore gang in Baltimore confronted me. He claimed to be a killer and threatened to kill me. He soon found out that although I was a Christian, I was not a soft one. I stood up and said, "I don't want to get kicked out of the program, but I will not let you hurt me. You want a fight? I'll give you a fight. I'm not afraid of you." We shouted at each other, our faces close. I became so mad, I could have bitten his nose off his face. He couldn't get me to back down, so he gave up and walked away, yelling words I won't repeat and criticizing my leadership style.

One of the things he said was, "You think you're perfect."

I walked back to my chair as a few of my peers praised me for standing up to the bully, but his final words rang in my ears. I questioned the Lord: *Was I unforgiving? Did my friendship come with such starched and rigid conditions? Was I, in some ways, failing my friends on Earth because I was so heavenly-minded?*

The Holy Spirit answered, "Yes, Charles. It's true. What are you going to do about it?" The gangster from Baltimore had meant our confrontation for evil, but God turned it into something I needed to make me a better person. I started listening more. I became a more compassionate friend, and over time I became a better leader. Most of all, I never forgot where I came from and how bad it had been for me. That gave me more compassion and patience for others.

JERRY

As my gratitude grew, I decided I would not only clean the bathrooms, but I would start doing the floors of the mission every month as well. I stripped off the old wax and applied new wax, refinishing all the floors on the first floor. At first, it was just me and my friend Jerry. Jerry was a chronic alcoholic who nearly drank himself to death. We got sober together, and early on, he was my only true friend. Jerry and I studied the Bible together and worked hard. He did not stand up to the bad guys with me, but he would listen to me, console me, and help me strategize.

Jerry came to the program with his third DUI, and the judge reduced his sentence by mandating him to spend forty-six weekends in the county jail. Because he couldn't drive, I drove Jerry to and from prison for the forty-six weekends. We grew close, having great chats as we traveled. We were sad when I had to drop him off, and there was always a crowd waiting with Jerry when I picked him up. I could hear them say, "Hey Jer, your friend's here."

One weekend, there was an epic blizzard. It hit after I had dropped Jerry off, and that following Sunday, the roads were impassable, but I took off anyway. I just kept imagining Jerry standing out there in the snow. If not for the signs and occasional light, you could not distinguish the country roads from the country fields. On top of that, I had to stop and clean the ice off the windshield wipers every few miles. I was so scared I would go off the road. Fortunately, I had a four-wheel-drive truck. Jerry had gone with me to the auction when I bought it.

I spotted the prison lights and pulled into the parking lot. Sure enough, Jerry and the other guys were huddled together for warmth. I didn't hear, "Hey Jer, there's your friend" this time because the blizzard was still howling. I leaned over to open the passenger door, and Jerry got in. He said, "I knew you would come." I'll never forget those five words or the tone in which they were spoken. He trusted me, and it felt good to be trusted by a friend.

Jerry and I worked hard together, and soon more guys took notice of the shiny floor. Some of the men recognized this as a marketable skill and wanted to learn the process. I delighted in teaching them how to strip, refinish, and spray-buff floors. It brought me so much joy, it hardly felt like work at all. One of the local churches that came to do ministry every month (we called them missionaries) also noticed the shiny floors and clean bathrooms. They asked a staff person, "Who does your floors and bathrooms? They look so clean all the time. Which company do you use?"

The man laughed and shouted, "We don't have a company! It's that guy over there, Knuckles." The church then proceeded to do something I've always thought was amazing. I don't know how they arrived at the decision, but those good people decided they would take a chance and hire me. Me! I was an addict in early recovery from one of the most devastating addictions. These good people gave the chance of a lifetime to a wretch like me.

People Believe in Me

Though I had graduated from the Christian rehab program, I still rarely felt like anyone believed in me. The staff seemed to prefer the white guys over the black guys, giving them preferential treatment. Until the white gentleman from Arkansas arrived, the only other staff member who was genuinely undaunted by race was the black director who had hugged me when I stumbled into the recovery center. There were very few black people on staff at this Christian ministry.

After I completed the year of rehab, I still had many wounds and an enormous load of self-doubt. I desperately needed others to believe in me and continued to volunteer at the center. Until I came to believe in myself, I had to borrow other people's faith in me. Both the tall director who had hugged me and the director from Arkansas told me they believed in me when I was about to give up. Hearing other people's faith in me made my spirit soar and my faith in God grow stronger. Now, I was being offered a full-time position at a church! A *church* was saying they had faith in me.

Another boost came after I graduated from rehab. The gentleman from Arkansas shocked me (and probably others) by inviting me to sit on his advisory board. Me, a recovered addict, on his board of advisors? I don't know if he ever knew how deeply he touched me. Inspired by his act of trust, when I later created a 501(c)3 nonprofit to provide mentors, all of them were alumni from the recovery program. I named us "The Alumni Group." We not only worked with the men still in the program, but we started street ministries in some of the most dangerous neighborhoods in the inner-city.

This was a staggering new reality for me: I was learning to accept the fact that other people, people I admired and respected, really believed in me. Like Jerry, they trusted me as a loyal friend. Like the directors, they appreciated my abilities and saw my worth and value as a leader and mentor. And now a whole church trusted me to keep their house of worship clean and in order!

I had emerged from the darkness into the light, and I saw an entirely different reflection of myself in the eyes of others.

You are … His own special people, that you may proclaim the praises of Him who called you out of darkness into His marvelous light.

1 Peter 2:9

YOU ARE ... HIS OWN SPECIAL PEOPLE, THAT YOU MAY PROCLAIM THE PRAISES OF HIM WHO CALLED YOU OUT OF DARKNESS INTO HIS MARVELOUS LIGHT.

1 PETER 2:9

CHAPTER EIGHT
LIFE IN THE CHURCH

After I graduated from the rehab, several factors got me through my first year of sobriety, but the biggest was being hired as the church custodian. The Wallingford Presbyterian Church could afford to hire anybody, so I was astonished when they wanted to interview me.

My interview with Reverend Dr. David Drain, who pastored and led the church, was my final hurdle in getting hired. Before the interview, my heart was pounding out of my chest. This man could put the kibosh on the whole deal if he wanted. When I entered his office, to my alarm, he shook my hand with a firm grip and held it for what seemed like an eternity. He looked me in the eyes with a stare that seemed to penetrate the depths of my soul. This man wanted to know who I really was, and I was scared he would not like what he saw.

Except for my ability to create shiny floors and clean bathrooms, things had not been perfect that year. Not everybody liked me. I'm not sure I even liked me! I thought for sure he would see everything I was before I came to Christ, all the ugly things I was and had done. Even as a Christian, I had so many flaws! What would those piercing eyes see?

As we sat down, he began with, "The missionary team speaks highly of you. I heard you are doing good things at the recovery center. What do you think makes you the right person for this job?"

I answered, "I work hard, and I am a self-starter. I'll always be on time and take good care of your place."

"It's good you are a self-starter because, as sexton, you will be your own supervisor." He was still looking straight at me, and I was a little intimidated, but I asked him what a sexton was. I had never heard the term before. He explained that the sexton oversaw the maintenance of all physical facilities of a church. Then he asked, "How do you get along with kids? We have a preschool here." I told him I was fine with kids.

The rest of the conversation is pretty much a blur in my memory. Still, there were two things embedded in my soul as I left that meeting: Giving me this job meant this man trusted me with part of the care of his church, his people; and this was a man I knew I could trust, someone I admired from that first handshake.

When Pastor Drain put the keys to the church in my hands and told me I was hired, I'm sure the whole universe heard my sigh of relief. I felt like he had saved my life. God surely must have been laughing, "So, you promised to clean bathrooms in Heaven? Well, here's your chance." After graduating, my first real job was cleaning bathrooms and floors in the most wonderful church I had ever seen.

This was a pivotal moment in my early recovery. I had just been rejected for an all-expenses-paid grant to a Christian college, and I was at a low point. I wanted to go to seminary badly, but there was only one grant offered, and the recovery center staff gave it to another resident. It felt just like high school all over again, and I lost confidence. I began hearing the negative voices in my head: "You're not college material. You're a loser. Nobody wants you." Sometimes, these voices seemed so loud that I couldn't hear God.

Interestingly, out of the three of us who graduated from the recovery program, two relapsed, and one of them had received the grant. When I wasn't picked, however, I felt like I was at the bottom again. Then

Pastor Drain hired me, and it wasn't long before I saw God's wisdom. Wallingford Presbyterian Church was to be my seminary and Pastor Drain and other church leaders my instructors.

God always blesses us beyond our wildest dreams. My imagination could never have come up with this plan. I'd never been in a church so beautiful. The good people of Wallingford Presbyterian Church invited me to become a member of their congregation. I took the new member classes, joined the church, and I've been a Presbyterian ever since.

As far back as I can remember, I had yearned and searched for a family I fit into, and this church turned out to be that family. I fit perfectly. There was no natural resemblance, of course, because they were white, and I was not. At first, I asked God if He was sure I was supposed to be there. Later, I could imagine His smile at that question! As I settled into my new life, I was never more sure or happy.

I was learning that, as you recover your life, you are surprised where God places you. I learned that He can handle your questions. And I also found out that whether or not He answered my questions, whether or not I understood what He was doing, I should just obey Him in faith. Trust Him.

Reverend Dr. David Drain

The first day I reported to work to clean the church, I noticed Pastor Drain's personal library in his office. There was a library down the hall from his office as well, which was for members, but Pastor Drain's books dealt with deeper issues. These were the books that piqued my curiosity. He studied fascinating authors, and he even had a very early and rare edition of the Alcoholic Anonymous *Big Book*.

One day, I got the courage to take down a book that had been catching my eye as I was dusting the bookshelf. I opened it and began to read. With the feather-duster in one hand and the book in the other, I dusted and read. The first chapter captured me. I reluctantly put it back where it belonged, desperately wanting to keep reading. That night, I could not stop thinking about that book. I tried to find it at the book store, but they told me it was out of print.

Finally, I came up with a strategy to read Pastor Drain's books. I would come in an hour earlier and clean so that everything would be perfect and spotless. Then I could take some time to read Pastor Drain's books. I knew I couldn't read first and clean later because I might lose track of time and not have my work done when Pastor Drain arrived. In this way, I could read his whole library, and he would never know. This went on for a while and worked well—until one fateful day, Pastor Drain came in early and found me at the table in his office, reading Donald Gray Barnhouse's *The Invisible War*.

I saw him, and my heart sank. I knew I was not supposed to be doing anything other than clean, and now the jig was up. I did not know what would happen, but I suspected that my dream job of cleaning the church was over. My previous life experience had taught me that he had every right to fire me on the spot.

To my amazement, as casual as you please, Pastor Drain started a conversation with me about the author and the book. Was this a setup? I was suspicious and happy at the same time. It seemed like we were reviewing the material, and he was testing my knowledge of the subject. I guess I passed, because suddenly he asked me, "You really like that book, Charles?"

"Yes," I replied, "I love it. But it's out of print. I haven't been able to find a copy of my own." Looking back, I think even though this was true, I might have been looking for mercy. I was sure the other shoe was going to drop.

Pastor Drain's tone turned serious, and my fear of being punished sent a shiver through me. Then, with those piercing eyes, he said, "If you like it, you can have it." Whoa! Did he say what I thought I heard? I never saw that coming! I was overcome, but I told him I couldn't take the book since it was signed and dedicated to him. He replied, "Still, take it. I would like for you to have it."

I could only respond, "I couldn't, Pastor Drain. It's yours."

"Well then, you can read it whenever you want." And that was that.

As I left his office, I believed in God's goodness as I had never believed it before—not because I thought He had gotten me out of a tight squeeze, but because I saw His heart in another human heart. For the first time, I believed God's people could really be like Jesus. And that included me.

Pastor Drain proved to be one of the most important people in my life. He encouraged me to learn, moving me toward the knowledge and wisdom I would need to help others. I sat in church, listening to his sermons, and took what I learned back to the mission. I taught others what he was teaching me. He may not have known he was my mentor, but he was.

I hope he knows how much I loved him. I would observe how he treated people and addressed matters, and I would try my best to be like him.

Not only was I encouraged to be a welcome part of the church family, but I had the joy of encouraging others. People would stop me in the halls or while cleaning the sanctuary just to talk. Some had problems they wanted to talk about, and some just wanted to hear my thoughts. I would put down my cleaning tools and give people my full attention. I never felt guilty or in trouble when Pastor David or Pastor Jeanne walked by and saw me talking to a parishioner. They never indicated this was anything but expected. I felt like the minister of cleaning, the minister with the mop!

Years later, a reporter was interviewing me in the women's bathroom as I was cleaning the toilet. I said, "There are times when I can't separate the work from the worship." It made her smile a big smile, and she wrote that in her article. I guess she was impressed that I could worship God and be thankful while cleaning a toilet. Little did she know how true this was!

I had always wanted a big family, and God gave me the most unusual one! In this new family, He made me useful, gave me a mentor and friends, and opened doors of opportunity for me to help others. I was overwhelmed again and again with the deepest heartfelt gratitude and love.

One day I told God, "I think this church will be the place I will work for the rest of my life." Looking back, I imagine God smiled once again, because He took me from the mop and bucket to behind a mahogany desk. But a lot happened before that came to pass! While I worked at the church, I also worked with men who had graduated from the same Christian recovery center as The Alumni Group or "TAG." We went into urban neighborhoods to minister to men who suffered from crime and addiction like we had.

We would set up on notorious corners and offer sandwiches and fruit drinks while preaching the Gospel and telling our testimonies. We helped men get their driver's licenses, jobs, and homes.

One church member, who was familiar with the law, coached me as I wrote the corporation bylaws and filled out the 501(c)(3) forms for TAG. A couple of members of the church became board members, and some helped us get into more churches to train men from the recovery center in floor care. We were able to pay men while they learned carpet care, tile care, and stripping and refinishing floors. The men were able to get fair-wage jobs after completing their training. Together, we had a good reputation for the work we did.

TAG brought the Lord's peace to troubled neighborhoods. We would go to the neighborhood church and ask permission to be a presence, offering prayer and testimonies on the worst corners. If they said yes, we would set up every Friday and Saturday evening. The group grew as we saw a tremendous success rate of maintaining sobriety in our men. Almost 100 percent of the men stayed sober. Many got married and had successful lives that included giving back to their neighborhoods as part of our group.

CHAPTER NINE

THE MIRACLE OF AA

You can look in the eyes of many addicted persons and see that they have surrendered to death. Their trauma and the addiction that resulted has devastated them. Intervention in this kind of surrender requires special skills, as it is difficult to rescue someone who is convinced that death is their only future. If you are called to do this kind of intervention, train well with experienced teachers and counselors. A counselor must have the discernment and skill to recognize different indicators in the speech and behavior of the client.

The thought process of the addict at this point is tantamount to suicide. They are convinced that only killing themselves will free them from their bondage and the darkness of the world they experience. I know because I was there. I literally could not imagine life without the drugs. At the same time, I was exhausted from living an addictive lifestyle. I wanted it to end. Death seemed a reasonable solution. Suicide made sense to me.

Cigarettes, drugs, alcohol, loveless sex, foul language, filthy humor—all these instruments of evil and destruction were my companions. In my own demented way, I thought I loved them more than anything else, even life itself. When buying food got in the way of buying drugs and alcohol, I stopped buying food. When my car insurance and repairs got in the way of drugs and alcohol, I sold my car. When rent got in the way of drugs and alcohol, I stopped paying rent and went homeless. I surrendered to inevitable death until death itself, suicide, appeared to be my deliverer.

> *But God will redeem my soul from the power*
> *of the grave: For He shall receive me. Selah.*
> *Psalm 49:15*

> *Trust in the Lord with all your heart,*
> *And lean not on your own understanding;*
> *In all your ways acknowledge Him,*
> *And He shall direct your paths.*
> *Proverbs 3:5–6*

I found the support I needed in my church and in the rooms of Alcoholics Anonymous. One of God's greatest gifts to the addict, a spiritual program that not only brings sobriety but joy in life, is the program called Alcoholics Anonymous and the many other programs for specific addictions based on it. That's why I want to spend an entire chapter devoted to it.

THE JOY OF ADMITTING POWERLESSNESS

I finally admitted I had no power over my addiction, absolutely zero. At the same time, I knew nothing would change if I weren't willing to change, and I could not do it alone. Admitting you are powerless is not a worldly concept; it is a biblical, spiritual truth that releases you from

BUT GOD WILL REDEEM MY SOUL FROM THE POWER OF THE GRAVE: FOR HE SHALL RECEIVE ME. SELAH.

Psalm 49:15

the bondage of trying to control your life and everyone and everything around you. You literally give up your human ability in exchange for God's supernatural ability. You are spiritually born again and no longer alone. You have a divine and Almighty Partner!

What I have just described are the first three steps of the 12 Steps of AA:

1. We admitted we were powerless over alcohol—that our lives had become unmanageable.

2. We came to believe that a Power greater than ourselves could restore us to sanity.

3. We made a decision to turn our will and our lives over to the care of God as we understood Him.

These first steps are often paraphrased: "I can't, He can, and I'll let Him." Again, they are simple but life-changing!

In Step 1, you could add my insert in brackets: We admitted we were powerless over alcohol [or any other addiction or bad habit]—that our lives had become unmanageable. Admitting we are powerless is the opposite of the self-help message. The self-help message makes a person the god of their life. They do everything in their own strength, by their own reasoning. Christianity says, "You are not the perfect God, and you cannot live a perfect life. But you can have a relationship with God that will transform you. All you have to do is get off the throne of your life and let Jesus sit there. Admit you are powerless, and let the One with all the power and wisdom be your Lord and Savior."

Like all the steps, which are biblical principles, steps 1 through 3 can be used in all healing processes, not just drug and alcohol addictions. In biblical terms, Step 1 is admitting that we are powerless to keep ourselves from sinning. Sin comes in many forms and disguises! Some people can't keep themselves from cheating on their spouse. Others can't keep themselves from stealing or lying to save their own skin. We all have our issues, and we all need God's help to overcome them.

The best thing about Step 1 is the admission. Admitting brings us to hope, which brings us closer to believing, which brings us closer to being willing, which ushers us into a relationship with the true source of the power to be free, Jesus. Step 1 may be the first time we admit the truth about our weaknesses and flaws. It opens the door to honesty, new viewpoints, and willingness to change.

I thank God I gave my life to Jesus at the beginning of my recovery but, for you, this change may not happen right away. Hang in there and keep moving toward God. Through Jesus, God forgives you of every sin: past, present, and future. He will not fail you! The first three steps inspire you to be honest, open-minded, and have a willingness to change in fundamental ways. Admitting you are powerless brings you closer to believing there is a God who can help you. Believing in a God who can help you brings you closer to being willing to let Him help you, and being willing to let Him help you ushers you into a relationship with the true source of your recovery from addiction.

As a Christian, the words in the Bible are spiritual food, alive and powerful, transforming me from the inside out. The same Spirit that raised Jesus from the dead, the Holy Spirit, lives in my new, born-again spirit, giving me the strength and wisdom I need for every situation. All I have to do is follow His lead, and He will keep me clean and sober. Do you see why the Gospel is called the Good News? And the first three steps of AA take you to it!

CONFESSION IS GOOD FOR THE SOUL

The Christian rehab program I attended was a fairly large facility that was poorly staffed. They barely acknowledged any of the steps but Steps 3, 4, and 5. It makes sense when you look at their religious background. The three steps are:

3. Make a decision to turn your will and your life over to the care of God as you understand Him.

4. Do a searching and fearless moral inventory of yourself.

5. Admit to God, to yourself, and to another human being the exact nature of your wrongs.

Step 3 (turn your will and life over to God) is a "come to Jesus" message. Step 4 (writing down your sins) is the gateway to living free of past sins, and Step 5 (confessing your sins) brings the joy and gratitude of forgiveness for your sins. These steps fit into a religious framework.

I knew nothing about the 12 Steps. When they told me to write down everything, I did. I didn't leave *anything* out. I truly thought, come confession time, I would sit in the elder's office and privately confess my whole heart and life. When I reported I was finished with my 4th Step list, I was led into a room of about 40 men, placed in front of a podium, and told, "All right, Charles. Let's hear it." This was my 5th Step!

My heart dropped. My mouth got dry as a desert. I looked around the room at all the eyes upon me. Now I knew why I was the only one to complete this step! But I also had the desperation of a drowning man who would do anything to get better. I started reading my confession, mumbling at first. The elder asked me to speak up, so I did. I told everything I thought I would *never* tell anyone—to a whole room of delighted, snickering men. They jabbed each other in the ribs, laughing and saying, "Did you hear that?" Even the elder had a look on his face that told me what he thought.

The class was dismissed, and the laughing men walked down the hall. The staff just disappeared. I think they'd heard way more than they asked for! Only four men waited at the door for me. They greeted me and thanked me. One said, "I thought that I was the only one that happened to." Another said, "I never dreamed there would be someone I could talk to about things like this." We spent hours in conversation, healing each other.

The 5th Step confession is supposed to be done with one trusted person. Putting me in front of a room of immature men was a terrible mistake that could have hurt me, but God redeemed this mistake. My relationship with Him was that I followed Jesus by obeying the authority He placed over me, and so Jesus made a way through the mistake to become a path of healing for me. He gave me my first taste of reciprocal ministry when he gave me those four men as friends. The Bible says it this way, "And we know that all things work together for good to those who love God" (Romans 8:28).

FORGIVING AND BEING FORGIVEN

When I discovered the 12 Steps of AA, I began participating in AA meetings and got a sponsor to help me. I saw how powerful the program was, how spiritual it was. The steps began with me getting honest with myself and God, then opening up to others with His help. My new friends in the rooms of AA helped me to complete the following four steps:

6. Become entirely ready to have God remove all these defects of character.

7. Humbly ask Him to remove your shortcomings.

8. Make a list of all persons you have harmed and become willing to make amends with them all.

9.. Make direct amends to such people wherever possible, except when to do so would injure them or others.

It's hard to forgive those who hurt you, but it is much harder to go to someone you have hurt, admit how wrong you were, and ask them to forgive you. In the end, sometimes they do, and sometimes they don't—but at least you can sleep at night, knowing you've done right by them and you can turn them completely over to God. You've done your part, and now you trust Him to do His part and heal them.

There are so many areas in the 12 Steps where the rooms of AA and my church family overlap. Good preaching and my brothers and sisters at church feed me spiritually and remind me who I am as a child of God. They lift me up and help me to live in more and more freedom, better able to do what God means for me to do. They help me undo what Satan did to and through me. He took a lot of years and used a lot of lost people to set a default in me that said, "Happiness comes from drugs, meaningless sexual encounters, foul language, and bad habits." To change those lies to the truth, I needed (and still need) a lot of saved, godly people to help me.

IT TAKES AN ARMY

If you think addiction just happens, then you have no idea why there are victims of addiction. Most people think the victims are those the addict hurt, that the addict is no more than a perpetrator. They don't see how the addict is the *primary* victim.

The business of addiction is one of the biggest moneymakers in the world. Farmers make their living growing opium, tobacco, and marijuana. Chemists make their living creating the finished products. Legal and illegal organizations make their living protecting and distributing these products worldwide. Addicts slave and steal for money to pay for the very thing that's killing them. There's an *army of evil* pointed directly at a person to get them addicted and keep them addicted; therefore, the recovering person needs an *army of good* to defend their recovery, their peace, their joy, and their life. The church and AA are where I found my army.

When I first got sober, I went to four AA meetings per week. I was a secretary in one, a general service representative in another, made coffee in another, and just listened to my elders in another. I continue to attend AA meetings to help others in recovery and to continue growing. I needed to be a part of their army, their fan club, and their recovery family.

What I'm describing are the last three steps, which are steps of maintaining and growing stronger in our recovery:

10. Continue to take personal inventory and when you are wrong promptly admit it.

11. Seek through prayer and meditation to improve your conscious contact with God, as you understand Him, praying only for knowledge of His will for you and the power to carry that out.

12. Having had a spiritual awakening as the result of these steps, you try to carry this message to alcoholics and to practice these principles in all your affairs.

I need meetings to continue dealing with my issues and relationships with God and others. I need people to bounce stuff off to see if my thinking is right. I also need to continue serving others who are in recovery, especially those who are just beginning. Giving and imparting what you have learned is what Jesus was all about. He imparted His wisdom and understanding, He healed the sick, He helped those in need, and at the Cross, He gave His life for us. He gave us everything He had.

I need church and AA meetings because I will always need my army. I will always need my army because there will always be an army of demons and people who are influenced by them fighting against me. With my church family and friends in AA, the final steps keep me thinking straight and close to God. They get me ministering to others what I have learned, helping others through the steps as a sponsor or friend. Going through the 12 Steps of AA is truly a miraculous journey!

A BIG STEP OF FAITH

The Christian program I graduated from was part of a network of Christian recovery programs, and the main branch was in San Jose, California. The staff at the main branch were having trouble with their recovery program and asked me to come out to be their new director.

I moved across the country and stepped into a foreign environment. My predecessor had done things quite differently than I did. The clients were used to punitive measures being levied against them at every turn. Knowing their pain and fear, I offered the grace I had received. For example, the previous director had told the men that to get things, they would have to "kiss the ring." In other words, the more they recognized him as king, the better they would be treated. I told the men from day one, "I am you, and you are me. We are no different, and you can do what I do—most of you probably better!"

Treating the men with respect, as someone who was also in recovery, made them more invested in their recovery.

As I stepped into this new role, I began a new season of my life. What I had learned on the streets of Philly, at the Christian rehab program, as a member and employee of the Wallingford Presbyterian Church, and as part of The Alumni Group. All that I had experienced and the truth I came to know set me free. Now, I began to impart to others, so they could get free and stay free also.

For me to stay free, I had to help others recover and continue my education. My task was to use every tool available to teach the men clinical and biblical methods of staying sober. Many had repeatedly failed because they thought being sober was their end goal. I had to gently show them the difference between sobriety and sobriety in Christ. The combination of sobriety and salvation is stronger, and those who have both live more successful lives.

"I AM YOU, AND YOU ARE ME. WE ARE NO DIFFERENT, AND YOU CAN DO WHAT I DO— MOST OF YOU PROBABLY BETTER!"

CHAPTER TEN

SURPRISED BY GRACE

After I arrived in San Jose, I studied for and obtained multiple certifications and a license to counsel people like me. It was a steep learning curve as I adjusted to my new position, but God's grace saw me through it. I was offered a big office upstairs, with big windows, but I took the small office close to the front door. The office was so small; it could hardly house my huge collection of books. It was a cramped space, but I took it because of its location. As men finally found whatever it took to reach out for help and walk through the door, I wanted to be right there to give them a hug and whisper in their ear, "We've been waiting for you." Grace would surprise them at the door.

Grace is not just letting a person off the hook for an infraction or a mistake. It's not dismissing the transgression. In recovery, grace means we learn together from the mistake without condemning punishment or kicking the client out of the program. For example, when men would fail to win my predecessor's approval, he would cancel weekend family visits. I, on the other hand, would plan big family visits called Family Day. My staff and church volunteers would set up games for the kids and spouses to play and win small prizes.

Addiction is a family disease, so before the games, there would be an educational piece presented by my staff and me. The families would learn about their loved one's addiction and how they could heal from their own wounds as well. To the families' delight, we would then schedule individual family sessions. Of course, the kids couldn't wait until the cookout and games began! On Family Days, I would use the men's shortcomings to teach them hard lessons in an impactful and positive way.

Instead of kicking the client out and putting them back on the streets if they relapsed, I would put them on a stricter recovery plan that included exploring what triggered the relapse. Then we would develop a plan of action for similar situations to avoid relapse in the future. I separated them from the more vulnerable clients by putting them in a different building. They were helped by older, more experienced clients, graduates, and staff. That was the structure of grace. Grace must always come with structure, or the client may see it as weakness, which it is not. Grace is a strength that inspires discipline.

Clients expect punitive responses when they relapse or make a mistake, but grace catches them by surprise and makes them more open to alternative paths forward. It facilitates a stronger recovery, as the surprise of grace is not easily forgotten. Grace builds affection and trust in relationships, which is vital to recovery.

Grace is so much stronger than the punitive measures that numb a person's sensibilities and beat them down. God's grace lifts people up and brings them to life. During my tenure as director in San Jose, God rescued hundreds of men and their families from addiction, and there's no telling how many others those people went on to rescue.

Nothing is ordinary about grace! God gives us what we *don't* deserve—His love, His forgiveness, and His favor. Punitive measures are ordinary, but grace is extraordinary. Grace shocks the person into seeing God's compassion and mercy, perhaps for the first time in their life. Grace inspires them to live their life differently.

But he said to me, "My grace is sufficient for you,
for my power is made perfect in weakness."

2 Corinthians 12:9

GRACE IS SO
MUCH STRONGER
THAN THE PUNITIVE
MEASURES THAT
NUMB A PERSON'S
SENSIBILITIES AND
BEAT THEM DOWN.

THE SOURCE OF GRACE

We can never take credit for grace. Grace is always of God. And without the grace of God working in us, we would have no grace for others. In the beginning of recovery, the recipient of grace may associate the gift of grace with a particular person, but eventually, they will see that person fail in some way. They will learn that the person who offered them grace did so because they had received grace from God, and they will realize that none of us are the source of grace. God is the source!

For by grace you have been saved through faith, and that not of yourselves; it is the gift of God, not of works, lest anyone should boast.

Ephesians 2:9

True grace connects the client to God in a real way. If a counselor or mentor takes credit for the grace given (a secular view), then the addict can turn this wonderful gift into a means of manipulation. If grace is human, then it can be controlled and worked by another human to get their way. The Christian counselor, mentor, and friend should always give God the credit, demonstrating how God showed His grace to them and His grace is passed on to the client.

We ask God for His grace because we have a limited supply. We can only do so much in our human strength, and then we become jaded and calloused. But God's grace is unlimited. We need His unlimited and continuous flow of grace in our lives to carry out the demanding and challenging ministry to the poor, to addicts, and to our homeless neighbors.

God is all-powerful, so grace comes from a place of strength, not weakness. It takes the power of God to give grace, to forgive the one who relapsed and hurt others. It takes inner strength to find the path of recovery in the midst of a relapse crisis. The fact that true grace comes from a place of strength will be challenged in the mind of the addict.

FOR BY GRACE YOU HAVE BEEN SAVED THROUGH FAITH, AND THAT NOT OF YOURSELVES; IT IS THE GIFT OF GOD, NOT OF WORKS, LEST ANYONE SHOULD BOAST.

EPHESIANS 2:9

They have only seen strength and authority from those who punish and cause more pain and suffering. They must continually be reminded to see that grace is stronger, as it gives them strength to get back into recovery after a relapse.

When I taught Relapse Prevention at the Christian recovery center in the Philadelphia area, the man running the program was a tyrant. He had strict rules, and everyone tiptoed around, scared to death of landing on the wrong side of this fellow. Having lived in the area for so many years, I knew a lot of the addicts. One middle-aged crack addict, whom I'll call Byron, was a good person who had made some bad decisions. Believe it or not, there are some addicts like this. They reach into a pile of logs to get something they believe will be good for them, and a venomous snake bites them. They are still a good person, but that doesn't change the snake bite, nor does it stop the poison from bringing destruction and heartache.

Byron had struggled with addiction for years, and when he finally came into the recovery center, I was so happy to see him! I knew he was a good guy, but he did not know what he was walking into. The recovery manager was in the middle of a power struggle. He was trying to establish dominance over the other staff members. The clients were in the middle of a tug of war. A staff member would make a decision; then the recovery manager would reverse it just to frustrate them.

One day, Byron was helping a staff member clean a room. There was a discarded pair of shoes in a trash can. Byron asked the staff member if he could have the shoes since they were much better than the pair he had. The staff member said, "Of course, you can have them." The recovery manager had a rule that the clients could only get the used clothing on Wednesday. It was Tuesday, so the recovery manager kicked Byron out of the program to teach the staff member a lesson!

Two weeks later, Byron was found dead in an abandoned house. There was no grace for Byron. The recovery manager was an addict too. He was not only addicted to power, but later we would discover he was addicted to opioids. I got to see firsthand how harmful the absence of grace can be.

Another example of the power of grace came when it was reported to us one of our former clients had relapsed on alcohol. In our spirits, we knew it was serious. We dropped what we were doing and headed over to his apartment. When we walked into the room, it smelled like death had claimed its prey. I looked down at him. His skin was grey, and his body appeared lifeless, but God's grace saved a life that day. We got him to detox and then back to the program for a refresher. He went on to become a case manager in recovery. There are dozens of stories from my tenure as director of rescue and recovery where God's powerful grace saved lives.

Grace must not be seen as a resource that comes from you. True grace comes from God, and they should thank God, not you.

When a person is given grace, they experience tremendous gratitude, and gratitude always needs to be expressed. So, gratitude leads to service. Then serving others inspires humility, and humility brings the client right back to God's love. As we love and serve others in humility, His love is perfected in us.

If we love one another, God abides in us,
and His love has been perfected in us.

1 John 4:12

IF WE LOVE ONE ANOTHER, GOD ABIDES IN US, AND HIS LOVE HAS BEEN PERFECTED IN US.

1 JOHN 4:12

CHAPTER ELEVEN

SPIRITUAL LIFE

One of the world's most famous psychiatrists, Dr. Carl Jung, told a patient that any further medical treatment for his alcoholism was pointless. Stunned, the patient asked if there was any hope. Jung told him his only hope was to experience a genuine conversion, a spiritual transformation. According to Jung, such experiences were rare for alcoholics, but those who had such a transformation often stopped drinking.

Most of the time, the client knows the answer and just needs to talk about it freely. We must always be ready for God to surprise us by the good work He does in a clinical session, whether we can mention Him or not; but in my experience working with others, spiritual life is essential to overcoming anything in life, especially addictions.

THE HOLY SPIRIT

As Carl Jung indicated, clients need a *spiritual* transformation, and that can only come through Jesus Christ. Jesus called it being "born of the Spirit."

Jesus answered, "Most assuredly, I say to you, unless one is born of water and the Spirit, he cannot enter the kingdom of God. That which is born of the flesh is flesh, and that which is born of the Spirit is spirit. Do not marvel that I said to you, 'You must be born again.' The wind blows where it wishes, and you hear the sound of it, but cannot tell where it comes from and where it goes. So is everyone who is born of the Spirit."

John 3:5–8

Being spiritually born again is more than a second chance; it is a brand-new life, lived from the inside out. When you are born again, the Holy Spirit resurrects your spirit from the dead and connects you to God the Father. The Holy Spirit now inhabits your spirit, and you know you are a child of God and eternal citizen of Heaven. Your identity is in Jesus, your destiny is in the Father, and your ability to overcome addiction or any other challenge in life freely flows from the Holy Spirit inside you.

Therefore, if anyone is in Christ, he is a new creation; old things have passed away; behold, all things have become new.

2 Corinthians 5:17

The Holy Spirit inside you becomes your Teacher, Instructor, Comforter, and Guide. Following the Holy Spirit in God's grace and ability is a lot easier than trying to keep a set of rules. I know alcoholics and addicts who have been in recovery for years, trying to follow a set of rules. Most of them are miserable. They are trying to transform

THEREFORE, IF ANYONE IS IN CHRIST, HE IS A NEW CREATION; OLD THINGS HAVE PASSED AWAY; BEHOLD, ALL THINGS HAVE BECOME NEW.

2 CORINTHIANS 5:17

themselves by behavior modification. They usually have a "higher power" who isn't Jesus Christ or the God of the Bible, so their "spiritual" life is actually an intellectual exercise.

The Holy Spirit transforms us from the inside out. He gives us a new nature that doesn't want to sin or displease God because we love Him and are so grateful to have eternal life and peace. The Holy Spirit is God's grace working in us to grease the wheels of all the changes we need to make in our lives. People who don't have God's grace have to rely on their own strength. They have no supernatural courage, wisdom, and strength to draw upon.

Those who haven't been born of the Holy Spirit are still walking in darkness, living in the confines of their natural thinking. It is very hard for them to get sober and stay sober. Those who take pride in and credit themselves for their sobriety usually find other addictions to take the place of drugs or alcohol. They smoke cigarettes like chimneys, drink coffee by the quart, and become workaholics. They are sober but don't live in real, lasting joy and freedom.

Where the Spirit of the Lord is, there is liberty.

2 Corinthians 3:17

Holy Spirit = Freedom. A hallmark of spiritual life is gratitude because the power of the Holy Spirit is actively setting us free from all the sins, fears, and bad habits that caused us heartache and tried to destroy our lives. The only lasting gratitude we can ever know is toward the God who saved us and sets us free from our addictions. The Heavenly Father is always the same. Jesus never changes. The Holy Spirit inside us is a constant reminder of their love and faithfulness. This reality offers the Christian a continuous state of gratitude, hope, and love in the midst of problems, difficulties, and tragedy. In short, the Holy Spirit is God's power!

Some people think they can find fulfillment and security in things like money, sex, position, and possessions—but these things are not eternal. These things don't last or stay the same. And they can turn on you! In fact, they can become addictions too. Any gratitude you have for these things is temporary. They bring fleeting emotions of happiness— like the heroin fix that doesn't last and leaves you craving more. But the Holy Spirit is eternally clean, clear, and powerful. He gives you a supernatural high, a freedom and security of being close to God that makes any other addiction or worldly affection look pale and lifeless.

Walk in the Spirit, and you shall not fulfill the lust of the flesh.

Galatians 5:16

Being born again spiritually is the greatest miracle a human being can experience, so of course, it will make an enormous positive difference in the life of someone in recovery. With the Holy Spirit inside them, they literally can draw upon God's divine power and wisdom to reject any evil craving and stay clean and sober. That divine power and wisdom lives inside them, in the person of the Holy Spirit.

DEALING WITH THE DEVIL

Those in recovery who have not been born of the Holy Spirit may sense evil and recognize the darkness they live in, but many do not understand that they have a spiritual enemy. Christians know the enemy is Satan, the devil, and they have to deal with him.

Satan hates God, so he hates all human beings because they are created in the image of God. He especially hates Christians because they are being conformed to the image of Jesus Christ, who soundly defeated him! I have tremendous gratitude that Jesus not only defeated Satan and his demons but gave us authority over them. We have the authority to kick the devil out of our lives and the lives of others in the name of the Lord Jesus Christ.

Then the seventy returned with joy, saying, "Lord, even the demons are subject to us in Your name."

And He said to them, "I saw Satan fall like lightning from heaven. Behold, I give you the authority to trample on serpents and scorpions, and over all the power of the enemy, and nothing shall by any means hurt you.

Luke 10:17–19

In this passage of Scripture, serpents and scorpions represent demons. Christians have authority over Satan and demons in the name of the Lord Jesus Christ. So, if we have all this authority, why do Christians stumble, mess up, or fall and relapse? Somewhere, somehow, they listened to and believed the lies of their spiritual enemies. A chief lie is, "You've got this." Pride and self-sufficiency are the enemy's worst work.

God loves obedient, loving, thankful hearts; the devil hates everything God loves. He is in the business of influencing people to be arrogant and totally self-centered. A Christian is God-centered, but Satan wants people to be self-centered. Then, he knows they are under his spiritual influence. The whole "self-help" movement is designed to keep a person away from Jesus Christ, who is the only way to know God and live a God-centered life—to walk in the freedom of the Holy Spirit and be free from all addiction by recognizing and renouncing the devil's lies.

Satan is the master of the counterfeit. He has false peace, joy, love—you name it. He is a copycat of everything good that God made. He perverts and distorts what God has created to be good. He is a liar and an expert at deceiving people. Christians must read, meditate, and study the Bible—the Book of Truth—every day to defeat him. We can memorize verses of Scripture and meditate on them when we don't have a Bible with us. Keeping our thoughts in line with the truth of God's Word enables us to recognize the lies of the enemy.

For example, self-help says, "You can do this. You have your truth, your power." But the Bible says, "We look to God for our help."

Jesus is the center of the believer's life, and with the Holy Spirit and the truth of the Bible, a believer can recognize and reject lies. It is a daily battle. It is in these battles that we who are free in Christ find opportunity. We don't shrink from opposition; instead, we use it much like a workout to grow our muscles of faith and gratitude. The stronger the opposition, the stronger the muscles grow.

As others watch us fight the good fight of faith while remaining thankful and joyful, they begin to wonder if they could ever have the same faith and joy. That usually leads to questions, and our answers lead them to the Lord. They are saved, begin amazing recovery, and have the joy of eternal life. Then the lies of the enemy can be crushed in their lives too!

Avoiding Partial Recovery

My brethren, count it all joy when you fall into various trials, knowing that the testing of your faith produces patience. But let patience have its perfect work, that you may be perfect and complete, lacking nothing.

James 1:2–4

Partial recovery is the clinical term that describes the opposite of being "perfect and complete, lacking nothing." In partial recovery, lacking is dangerous. You will not learn this in a 30-day secular rehab and maybe not even in a Christian one. If you do not believe addiction is sin and sin is separation from God, or have no desire to know God, then spiritual life is nonsense to you. As a result, you will most likely come out of rehab having achieved only a partial recovery.

Why am I making a big deal of this? You may be sober but have no idea who you are and what you were created to do. If you don't know who you are or have an internal, God-given sense of value and purpose, you may become negative, discouraged, and depressed, and likely relapse. Knowing how God loves you, values you, and has a purpose for you keeps you grateful, uplifted, and not likely to relapse.

It is important for clients to be taught the value of spiritual life, especially in Christian rehab programs. It's sad when even Christian facilities don't preach the Gospel and show how the 12 Steps of AA are taken from the Bible. Romans 1:16 says that the Gospel is the *power of salvation*, which means being whole in spirit, soul, and body. Nothing partial about it!

Unfortunately, secular clinicians have promoted what amounts to a partial recovery, which is really just plain lazy. They call it "Harm Reduction" recovery, and the government is buying and selling it too. These programs keep the addict in the system and give them no promise of freedom. Why? It keeps the money rolling in! Many clinicians hustle it, and addicts sign on to it because no one tells them there is something better. It's big money, it's easy, and it's the way of the world.

On the other hand, partial recovery can also happen when a Christian recovery program does not provide all the teachings and activities needed. For example, nonprofit Christian recovery centers can focus on work therapy (where clients work to keep the center going) and neglect recovery training and counseling. They do this to save money and because they are understaffed. Sometimes, even unconsciously, they are more interested in raising money than getting their clients the proper care and training.

This was my rehab experience, but if the client is like me and has a strong desire to get sober by pursuing a relationship with Jesus Christ, they still can make it. They must avoid resentments over heavy work schedules, embrace the work, and serve God in it. Clients in these situations, like me, must find a good sponsor and a strong spiritual mentor. Then they can continue to pursue their faith and recovery even after they finish their rehab program.

A SERVANT'S HEART

One of the most important parts of recovery is service to others, which is a spiritual principle that has always been a part of church life and the AA program. Service was a joy for me because I was so grateful for my salvation. Jesus was the greatest servant of all, and I wanted to be like Him. I have seen many men's lives changed as they served others. John was one of the most striking examples.

A young, handsome, and highly intelligent man, John had every reason to be proud and in control of his life, to believe that he was okay. Nevertheless, he came to us broken and hopelessly addicted. Having associated with some pretty hard-core people, he had been in a lot of trouble, committing some of the worst crimes you can imagine. Luckily, he had a wealthy uncle who loved him and would do anything to help him change his life. He also knew that if John did not change, he would die.

When John's uncle asked me to bring John into my program, the young man passed all the screening procedures. However, he had a stash of drugs that he forgot he had hidden in a shoe. A few weeks into the program, he stumbled across the stash and immediately charged into my office with it. He said, "Mr. Knuckles, I had this Suboxone in my shoe. I found it, and I want to get rid of it." He assured me he wasn't using it or trying to be sneaky.

This was a significant breakthrough! John didn't have to confess. He could have hidden the drugs or thrown them away on his own, but he was showing me something different. Up until then, he had been operating on borrowed faith from the people who surrounded him. He had a great mentor who was a volunteer, along with other strong Christian men who were volunteers and modeled faith. But when he came to me with the stash from his shoe, he owned *his* faith. He trusted God that if he did the right thing, he would continue to grow and get better.

There was something about John that made me want to work with him, and I involved him in a program that would reveal his God-given gift of service. I took a team of men from the center to wash the feet of our homeless neighbors, a practice I wish more clinical directors would adopt. At every homeless camp, we would feed the people and wash their feet. We gave them sandwiches and drinks, new socks, and slightly used donated shoes. Lots of the guys from the recovery center volunteered to help, but most of them just wanted to get out of the center for a while. They weren't so willing to serve meals—or wash people's feet! I would pick the men I thought needed the experience to serve others, then pray the experience would make a difference in their recovery.

I have a pretty good street sense of people, and one of the measures of a man is his willingness to serve people he wouldn't ordinarily talk to. I decided to take John to a serving event, and at first, he was just happy for the distraction. Then he began to watch me as I caringly washed the feet of our homeless neighbors. I engaged them in conversation, trying to learn more about them, and I was transparent about my recovery and life as a believer.

As I was about to wash another man's feet, I heard a meek voice ask, "Mr. Knuckles, can I wash his feet?" I smiled before turning around because I knew the Holy Spirit was at work in John's heart.

Although my heart was exploding with joy, I calmly answered, "Yes, John. Please do." Right before my eyes, I saw the gift of service give John humility, which is the key to gratitude. From that time on, he began to immerse himself in service. He spotted a rat-infested space filled with old cardboard and cleaned it out. As the rats scurried, many of the other men in his group ran like little children, but not John. He was fearless in service and didn't stop until he got the job done. He cleaned up homeless campsites overtaken by trash and led teams of men to clean up polluted creeks. He was unstoppable!

John graduated from the program and went on to college. He became an amazing businessman and married a beautiful and equally gifted woman. John and his wife took serving to heart, and they opened their home to provide encouragement and guidance to groups of young people who needed to find their way.

Humility is one of the glorious by-products of service, and it is also a key to the Father's heart. John still washes his homeless neighbors' feet, just like Jesus. Service taught John humility, humility gave him gratitude, and gratitude inspired him to help others even more. There is nothing more spiritual than serving others!

LIFE WITH THE SAINTS

A 2015 survey by researchers at the London School of Economics and the Erasmus University Medical Center in the Netherlands found that participating in a religious organization was the only social activity associated with sustained happiness—even more than volunteering for a charity, taking educational courses, or participating in a political or community organization. It's as if a sense of spirituality and an active, social religious practice were an effective vaccine against the virus of unhappiness.

This is a quote from *Time* magazine's special edition, "The Science of Happiness," written by Bryan Walsh. Research shows that the happiest people tend to be religious, married, and reasonable, with high self-esteem, job morale, and modest aspirations.

After rehab, when I began my work as sexton of the Wallingford Presbyterian Church, I quickly became a functioning member. I already knew many of the members through their work at the center. They captivated me with their hard work for poor people in the neighborhood. To me, they reflected almost everything Jesus was and is, as described in Romans 5:8, "But God demonstrates his own love for us in this: While we were still sinners, Christ died for us." In my mind, if I wanted to be more like Jesus, I should hang out with these people.

I always attribute the church to saving my life. They took my recovery far beyond where the rehab dropped me off. The church knew little about addiction, but they knew everything about redemption and recovery for all people, no matter their issues. Jesus is the only way a human being can be redeemed and recover from the effects of sin.

Among my brothers and sisters in the church, while learning more about Jesus, I found acceptance, purpose, worth, happiness, well-being, and joy among my brothers and sisters in the church. They gladly let me borrow these qualities from them until I established my own and stabilized my emotions, feelings, and moods. It became clear to me that Jesus gave me a purpose, and the church gave me a base of operation for that purpose. If you can find a church that serves people in need, preaches the Word of God, and encourages you in your family and profession, that's where you want to land.

LET'S DO IT RIGHT!

Mahatma Gandhi once said, "I like your Christ. I do not like your Christians." That statement does not anger me; it challenges me. Like Gandhi, I say to secular clinicians, "I like your mental health knowledge. I do not like your mental health systems." Centers for recovery cannot go the distance in encouraging a client to become whole in spirit, soul, and body without the spiritual element. And from what I have experienced and witnessed, the spiritual life with God through Jesus Christ is the most vital part of recovery. A redeemed spirit in a relationship with God is the foundation for a healthy soul and body.

I know of some Christian recovery centers that cannot be licensed, but they are very successful at what they do. I even know judges who will risk reprimands to send a chronic addict to a Christian facility because they know they won't get the help they need in a secular program. Why is this happening? There is only one reason: Government regulations and the media-driven culture shuns anything Christian-oriented. I pray there will be a time when government-based recovery would accept Christian-based recovery, recognizing Christian clinicians bring something powerful to the battle against addiction. I pray they discover how many highly skilled Christian clinicians are hobbled by government restrictions concerning the faith their clients need to have a successful recovery.

It is said in recovery, "If the addict is not interested in recovery, there's nothing you can say right; but if the addict is truly ready for recovery, there's little you can say wrong." I take sayings like this with a grain of salt, because it denies the miracle power of God and can turn good counselors into lazy ones. We should always do our best to pray

A REDEEMED SPIRIT IN RELATIONSHIP WITH GOD IS THE FOUNDATION FOR A HEALTHY SOUL AND BODY.

and give the best counsel, maintaining enthusiasm for each person who is struggling to live. But only God knows the word or phase of truth that will cause a spark in the addict's brain, fill their heart with a new vision, transform them from helplessness and lethargy to hope, and give them the will to live and thrive.

When a client enters into spiritual life with God through Jesus Christ, they not only have a Heavenly Father to lean on, but the relationship is two-way. God wants and is fully able to turn difficult and trying situations into blessings to transform the client's heart and soul. He prepares them for things ahead and heals the hurts of the past, and the Holy Spirit inside then strengthens, imparts wisdom, and gives comfort. Therefore the most effective recovery programs are always spiritual and Christian.

CHAPTER TWELVE

CHILDHOOD TRAUMA IN VULNERABLE ADULTS

Whether it is sexual abuse, physical abuse, or emotional abuse, childhood trauma often leads to addictive behavior in adults. I am confident that I am not the only survivor of these traumas. I know how our past can hinder recovery from addictive behaviors such as gambling, spending money, sex outside of marriage, binging and purging food, hurting our bodies, alcoholism, and drug addiction. People who have experienced childhood traumas can also develop Obsessive-Compulsive Disorder (OCD), anxiety, depression, and Post Traumatic Stress Disorder (PTSD). I only specialize in recovery from addiction, but the tools and methods in recovery from addiction can help a person heal and be free from other disorders and issues as well.

Childhood trauma manifests many ways in an adult. Mine manifested as drug and alcohol addiction, anxiety, depression, and

PTSD. I still navigate the psychological issues to this day. Like my addiction to drugs, they are not cured but are managed by the lifestyle I have adopted. In my case, depression is probably the worst. It comes in waves, and it rears its ugly head, especially on holidays. I react to holidays differently than most people. I become more reclusive and, unless encouraged, I avoid social events. In the past, I would go to AA meetings and hike the beach alone.

Close friends often include my wife and me in a special Christmas celebration. I thank God for them, because otherwise I would send my wife to her family for Christmas and stay home alone, doing nothing. A tree would remind me of how dismal Christmas was for me as a child, with no gifts, special meal, or the gathering of a loving, happy, extended family.

I get depressed when I think about the past. It overpowers me at times, and since it is a familiar place, I am tempted to stay there. Activity with friends helps me emerge from it, but since I'm an introvert, I must force myself into group activities. PTSD causes physical symptoms that heighten my awareness, and I get panic attacks that, fortunately, I have learned to manage. Anxiety haunts me when I am called to do something challenging, like speaking engagements or visiting friends.

Once, I was going to attend a men's meeting but started feeling anxious and depressed. I thought the group of men were out of my league. I started obsessing about what they would think about me and whether they would like me. I stayed in the parking lot across the street, spying on the men as they went into the building. I was afraid to cross the street. I finally pushed myself to cross that street and walk up to the group. Right away, one of the guys hugged me, and the anxiety waned, simultaneously replaced by joy. I thank God He gave me the strength to get myself out of my delusion.

My friends often tell me they care about me, and when I confess my fears to them, my anxiety melts away in their love. In turn, I can show my clients the same care. It's been said, "People don't care how much you know until they know how much you care." I'm there for them. I try not to break appointments. I listen to them and recall what I've heard later, reviewing my notes of previous meetings before the next meeting. I sometimes share my struggles and how I am recovering, so they can relate to me more easily and not feel like they are in it alone. It also helps to take groups offsite to cookouts, movies, bowling, softball games, and hikes. All this strengthens and encourages a new, godly view of who they are and what they can accomplish in relationships and work.

MALICIOUS CODE

Sexual, emotional, and physical abuse to children inflicts systemic damage. The devil influences people to mistreat the child, and in the process, a malicious code of lies and deception is placed in the child's thinking. This malicious code corrupts, distorts, and twists every area of the victim's being into a life God never intended for them.

From what I understand about malicious code in computers, it is a security breach that cannot be fixed by conventional antivirus software. You need an expert who knows the operating system and can go deep into it to remove the destructive code. I think it's safe to say childhood trauma is a malicious code that can only be removed by an expert, someone who knows the victim better than anyone else. God made them, and He is the expert they and their counselors, mentors, and friends need. He knows how to chip away at the malicious code and replace it with love, truth, peace, joy, purpose, and fulfilling relationships.

This is the point I try to make to both clinical and spiritual counselors in dealing with childhood trauma: You must turn to God to know the steps to take to help someone break free of the deathly grasp of childhood trauma. I know this is true because I still fight this diabolical code and can only defeat and expel it with God's and other counselors' and friends' help. For example, if I have suicidal thoughts stemming from the malicious code that runs through my brain, they will include: "You are not loveable. You are different in a bad way. You can never be a normal person. You will always want what's bad and can never desire what's good. You are incapable of making good decisions. You can only hurt people." And on and on it goes until I stop it and remind myself what God thinks of me, which is who I really am.

For someone who has never been severely traumatized as a child, having a relationship with a person who has these kinds of traumas in their background is difficult. Particularly in the beginning of recovery, we cannot process emotions as a normal person might, and it is difficult for family and friends to understand this. Loved ones may encourage us either gently or emphatically to "just get over it." They care genuinely for us, but they cannot imagine why we continue to fall. That's why family and friends must be educated about their loved one's recovery. It is why I believe recovery is a family and church community affair.

The malicious code sets us up to fail because it is all lies, and we have believed the lies since childhood. A foundational belief is that we are unlovable, so we automatically question motives when a person or group expresses care for us. They must be crazy or have some devious agenda—because we are not loveable! What do they want from us? When will they hurt us? We don't choose to be cynical or doubtful and we don't want to hurt others, but it's written into our twisted survival instinct. It's hard to imagine good because we never experienced good as children, and if we did experience good, it was soon followed by betrayal and pain.

In order to help us, people must cut through our defensive systems and penetrate our protective walls. If they want a relationship with us and desire to help us, there's a lot of reparative work ahead of them. And, quite frankly, most people find it hard to sustain caring long enough to facilitate healing. We are also a busy culture, and we lose many vulnerable people, not because we don't care but because we have grown so busy that we've become dull and insensitive.

A WORD FOR COUNSELORS

We live in an overworked culture: the more clients, the more money. Often, quality of care is lost in a system based on making a profit. Counselors are overloaded with clients. Sometimes, counselors stop caring and just go through the motions; for these counselors, this would be a good time for them to take a break, retire, or find another job. Addiction counselors, or counselors and therapists in any field, have to continually monitor themselves. In some situations, they may have difficulty caring for all their clients because of the enormity of their caseloads, experiencing burnout or compassion fatigue. If not careful, they can injure themselves, which leads them to injure their clients. This is especially important when counseling victims of childhood trauma. It is often the hardest work we do; it is extremely emotional, and it takes a lot of prayer, thought, patience, and perseverance.

My assistant counselor and I started counseling an entire family. Addiction is a family disease, so we saw this need for one client's family in particular. We began seeing all the family members and worked out a treatment plan for them. It worked so well, another family made a request for appointments. The clients passed the word to the rest of the residents that the family counseling worked. Before we realized it, my assistant and I were overloaded. We were the only licensed counselors, so there was no one to share the load. None of the families could afford the service, so we did it for free. For our own health and quality of care to our clients, we had to limit ourselves to two families for 90 days at a time.

With all clients, but especially those with childhood trauma, you must be transparent. My clients see that I also have an army to help me stay sober and fight all the malicious codes that try to destroy my relationships and zap the life out of me. I tell them about my church and how important it is to me. I encourage them to become active members of a church. Make coffee and bring food. If they are able, do childcare, teach Sunday School, and serve on committees and boards.

I tell them how the church is a safe and reliable way to find out how a healthy relationship works. As I hear the truth of God's Word and interact with believers who genuinely love and care for me, it chips away at the lies of being unloved and worthless. I openly share how I overcome the effects of childhood trauma.

Community and support groups are like a mirror that reveals who you were created to be and what you were created to do. As you get stronger and more "yourself," you help others do the same. You discover who you really are. You are not unlovable. You are loved by God and His people. You are a valuable and needed member of the church, as well as all your support groups. And you have gifts and abilities that enable you to be a welcome member of society.

People who can't trust anyone are desperate to find a counselor, a friend, or a mentor who actually lives the lifestyle they advise others to adopt. So, counselors and friends, take good care of yourself as a healthy model for those you help. Let them see you love them as you love yourself, all because of God's love for you and them. This is key to destroying malicious codes and replacing them with loving truth.

Stephen Minister Russ

The Presbyterian Church has a group called Stephen Ministers, trusted and mature laypeople who supplement pastoral care. The program teaches laypeople to provide one-on-one care for individuals who request support. They are trained to listen to and help the individual process their feelings in a healthy, biblical way. When I came to the church, I requested a Stephen Minister and was fortunate to receive Russ.

Russ was a retired gentleman who wanted to do more for people in need, so he trained to be a Stephen Minister. He worked with me for almost two years. Stephen Ministers also receive support as they minister to others. They meet both with their care receiver and their team weekly. When they meet with their team, they pray together, compare notes (without revealing the identity of their clients), and strengthen each other with observations and encouragement.

Russ knew absolutely nothing about addiction, which turned out to be exactly what I needed. Even though I was an addict, I didn't always need to talk about addiction; sometimes, I just needed to talk about how I felt. Other times I wanted to hear and witness Russ' more normal life events, which gave me something to hope for.

Over time, I realized I could trust Russ, so I grew more and more transparent and vulnerable with him. In some ways, talking to my Stephen Minister was more of a safe place than the Christian rehab program. That's one of the main reasons I recruited Christian mentors for each client when I became director of a recovery program. Through my relationship with Russ, I discovered that my addictions were an outward manifestation of the inward emotional trauma I had suffered. I saw addiction through a different lens as a means of managing (actually mismanaging) my emotions. Because of this, I could more easily talk about my feelings with Russ.

On a deeper level, I discovered that Russ was a model of a well-balanced man. He modeled, and I observed. I am a visual learner. I needed that model right in front of me so I could watch how he managed himself. Like most childhood trauma victims, the cynic in me tried to pick Russ apart. I tested him early on, telling him shocking truths about me that I was sure would cause him to abandon me. He didn't. He just showed up the next week with a good attitude.

I would hear the announcement over the P.A., "Charles Knuckles, you have a visitor in the cafeteria." There was Russ, the true and genuine model of masculinity I needed to see. In many ways, he showed up like Jesus and did not lie to me, betray me, or forget me. He did not mock me or ridicule my absurd beliefs. If he did laugh at something I said, it was always a gentle laugh and only when appropriate—after all, some of the stuff I said and did was outrageous! I thank God for Russ, who helped me to see and come to trust a Heavenly Father who loved me through and through. That truth stripped away the malicious code, the lies that I was unlovable and worthless, and I began to heal.

I am reminded of a passage in Matthew 17:14–21, when the disciples asked Jesus why they could not cast out a demon from a boy.

Jesus told them to reject unbelief and simply have faith in Him and His Word, that even faith the size of a mustard seed would do. He corrected them and then gave them some very valuable information. He said, "However, this kind does not go out except by prayer and fasting." I've come to a similar understanding of addiction, especially in those of us who have experienced childhood trauma.It takes more than one thing to cast out the demons and lies that try to destroy our lives. Yes prayer and fasting but also sponsors, mentors and other Christian disciplines.

First John 4:18 says that perfect love (God's love) casts out all fear. Childhood trauma breeds paralyzing fear, which suppresses emotion and warps reasoning ability, leading the victim to all kinds of addictive behaviors. Understanding the reality of God's love for them, choosing to believe He loves them, and daily receiving of His love—no matter what is going on in their life—is key to becoming whole from any kind of childhood trauma.

CHAPTER THIRTEEN

THE FIGHT FOR EMOTIONAL MATURITY

Human beings are blessed with many emotions, but oftentimes our primary choices are based on fear. Fear is good in its proper context, telling us not to do something dangerous, but when unhealthy fear becomes the dominant emotion, it denies us freedom and joy.

Addictions drown us in fear. An addict's brain is in constant fight-or-flight mode. We are afraid people won't like us, that we won't fit in, that we can't do a job. There are fears of getting caught, being exposed, and not having enough money to buy drugs to keep us from the pain. These are just a few specific fears that bear down on the addict. Not only is the constant fight-or-flight mode exhausting, but it also robs us of the life we should be living.

Upon hearing about the recovery center I was overseeing in San Jose, a young addict named Wayne made his way up from South Los Angeles.

He was at the end of his rope. He believed everyone he met instantly hated him, and everyone he already knew also hated him. Because of his small size, he was often targeted as easy prey and had been beaten many times. Bullies constantly robbed him. Unfortunately for him, his family life was no better, as his dad was seriously abusive.

One day I took Wayne and some of the other men to a movie. It was a good movie, so the theater was crowded. I noticed he was frightened of the people around him. As I was buying popcorn and drinks, he walked up to me with a panicked look on his face. He had tears in his eyes and his whole body shaking. He said in an eerie whisper, "Mr. Knuckles, there are sooo many people."

I put my arm over his shoulders and replied, "It's just you and me, Bud. Let's enjoy the movie and this popcorn." The rest of the men never teased Wayne. They just came around him as brothers in Christ, giving him the support he needed. I encouraged the men in the "each one teach one" mentoring model. I would tell them, "Even if you've only been here for a week, when you see a new guy, show him how you got through that week."

About six weeks later, Wayne was so confident, he was speaking in class. He had some good things to say. He had borrowed faith, hope, and gratitude from his brothers until he owned them. We all loved Wayne through his self-doubts and fears, and through our love, he recognized God's love for him. Wayne found out all about a God who loved him so much, He would never leave him.

One day I took the men on a long hike, and we stopped to rest under a vast group of redwood trees. Wayne and his band of brothers made a commitment that no matter what, they would be there for each other. With the help of his brothers, Wayne was going to be just fine. He had to learn to navigate some emotions he had anesthetized over the years because of the fear and pain. But with his sober friends' encouragement and learning how others processed their emotions, he opened his heart to the unfamiliar in order to be healed.

The more we can manage fear and keep it in its proper place with our other emotions, the more freedom we enjoy. Fear plays an important part when used correctly, but when it is out of control, even slightly, we lose freedom. I personally think that everyone battles some form of addiction and struggles with their own fears. Many of us are addicted to our fears and don't realize it. Someone once said, "If you fear God, you won't fear anything or anyone else." Fearing God is acknowledging He is in charge. This is a healthy fear involving reverence and respect. And the Bible tells you the Creator of the Universe loves you! He is not a cruel taskmaster; He is a lover of your soul. He wants to deliver you from dysfunctional fear and give you joy, courage, and success.

Fear of God is also faith in God. When you recognize God is sovereign and put your trust in Him, He proves He is faithful to you—which increases your faith in Him and decreases your fear of everything else. I put my life in His hands, and He took away my desire for cigarettes. He began to deliver me from the habits of thinking and behavior that came from debilitating fear and brought nothing but destruction. Every step of faith I have taken with Him, no matter how painful or scary it seemed at the time, brought me into more and more freedom.

SOBER BUT IMMATURE

When I started using drugs at eighteen years old, I stopped developing emotionally. Medical research has shown this to be true of alcoholics and addicts. When I entered recovery at forty-nine years old, I was emotionally immature. When I became sober, my previously anesthetized emotions overwhelmed me, like a tsunami landing on a defenseless island. The slightest disapproval from anyone would send me into fear and condemnation. The old fears ignited the old anger, which would go from zero to one hundred in seconds. Mentally, I would strategize my defense to the perceived offense in a hundred battle scenarios.

Then there was love. As a client, if an attractive volunteer gave me a slightly larger portion of food than the guy before me in the chow line, I thought she was attracted to me and would dream of love. Of course, I would never act on any of these imaginations, but I felt like I was traveling through an emotional obstacle course. I had to find a

EVERY STEP OF FAITH I HAVE TAKEN WITH HIM, NO MATTER HOW PAINFUL OR SCARY IT SEEMED AT THE TIME, BROUGHT ME INTO MORE AND MORE FREEDOM.

way to occupy myself, so I dove into work. Work helped me stop the accusations of the enemy, while my brothers, counselors, and mentors in Christ coaxed me to continue to deal with my emotions and grow up.

Emotional immaturity is a breeding ground for misinformation and a primary reason for relapse. Relapse is an emotional decision nestled in misinformation supported by emotional immaturity. Emotional immaturity is called Low Emotional Intelligence, or Low EQ. For example, emotional immaturity can generate a powerful resentment that says, "You have every right to get high! Look what was done to you!" Recognizing and facing emotional immaturity is vital for successful recovery, and this is one thing you can't do alone. You need someone or a group to be your mirror, to show you the faulty reasoning, expose the resentment, and bring you to a place of repentance and forgiveness. That's growing up emotionally.

Emotional health can be confused with mental health, but they are distinctly different in that what you feel and what you think may not be in sync. I may feel like I want to get high, but my brain thinks it is a bad idea. On the other hand, I may reason my way into believing I can take one drink and be okay, but my emotions are suddenly insecure and wary. My emotional instinct is formed from poorly interpreted experiences.

Feelings and thoughts are intimately connected. In fact, sometimes one influences the other, for good or bad. The key to becoming emotionally and mentally mature is the same: Act on what you know to be true and trust God. Jesus said it is the truth that sets you free, and the truth is what God says in His Word. This is why it is so important for new believers, whether in recovery or not, to learn to live their lives reading, studying, and living according to God's Word.

Then Jesus said to those Jews who believed Him, "If you abide in My word, you are My disciples indeed. And you shall know the truth, and the truth shall make you free."

John 8:31–32

God's truth sets us free, sometimes in an instant and sometimes little by little. However, it is always miraculous!

There are so many unnecessary casualties and relapses in early recovery because of the waves of emotion an unprepared, vulnerable addict experiences. They desperately need support because they lack emotional maturity. They are so far out of their comfort zone. After spending years running from our emotions, escaping them through an addictive substance or behavior, it often takes years of sobriety for our emotional maturity to catch up to our age. We have run from and sometimes suppressed the memories of our past, so we have denied God the opportunity to address those memories with His truth—which will set us free. As we find the courage and strength in Him to face our horrible memories, reliving all those terrible feelings is usually a painful and often frightening process. In the end, the Holy Spirit exposes all the lies with the truth of God's Word until bad memories have no more power over us. And even if they do from time to time, the new reservoir of truth in us will remind us that in Jesus Christ, we are free of that thing. The more freedom we gain, the more mature we become emotionally.

Managing Emotions

Because I specialize in men's recovery, I may be out of my depth when talking about women's recovery. Women's emotions may require different methodologies for healing and maturity. For example, it's been suggested that women talk more freely about their emotions, while men typically do not talk about their feelings or how they process a particular emotion. People often speculate on the differences between men's and women's emotional maturity, but I try not to do that. I work with men according to the premise, "What happened is not nearly as important as to how we respond to what happened. How we respond is the only thing we can control." In the end, I think this concept is critical in navigating emotions for both men and women.

Emotions are largely a product of our lifestyles. Lifestyles may or may not help manage emotions, as they can be orderly or chaotic. In

GOD'S TRUTH SETS US FREE, SOMETIMES IN AN INSTANT AND SOMETIMES LITTLE BY LITTLE. HOWEVER, IT IS ALWAYS MIRACULOUS!

recovery, we must learn a healthy routine that incorporates managing our emotions. A healthy lifestyle includes avoiding all drugs except in the most critical situations. Another problem facing addicts in recovery is clinicians further anesthetizing their emotions through more drugs: psych meds or opioid substitutes. Desperation will make the client comply, but the drug substitutes only remind them of their drug of choice and often delay or hinder dealing with emotional responses. It's just a matter of time before they come to the place where they decide to relapse. There must be a major change in an addict's lifestyle, a daily life without drugs and alcohol.

In some clinics, using maintenance drugs becomes a vicious cycle, and a lot of money is involved. Keeping a client on a maintenance drug keeps them dependent on the clinic, which often receives government assistance for the drugs and care of the client. In this way, taxpayers are enabling addictions, and the clients are caught in an emotional purgatory. On the other hand, if clients can learn to manage the floods and waves of their emotions without drugs, they can survive the worst life throws at them and become emotionally mature.

We should always ask those in recovery to describe their emotions and never assume we already know. A good counselor will become familiar with the client's emotional patterns. Ask questions like, "How does that make you feel," or "Why do you think it made you feel like that?" Gently but firmly get them to open up. Give continuous, encouraging feedback by nodding your head, giving them your full attention, and voicing, "yes," "what else," or "go on."

There are interviewing techniques to manage emotions that involve a lot of listening. Once again, minimum training is needed. As a counselor, mentor, or friend, you can listen and ask open-ended questions to keep the conversation going. This is why community is so important. Even for a skilled clinician, listening is the most crucial part of their job. If the average addict could afford a therapist for several years, they would stand a chance at figuring out how to manage their emotions on their own, but most people I know can't afford that.

There are counseling techniques available for controlling emotional responses in both secular and Christian Emotional Intelligence literature. Although the term Emotional Intelligence first appeared in a 1964 paper by Michael Beldoch, author, psychologist, and science journalist Daniel Goleman's 1995 book, *Emotional Intelligence*, brought the terms EI and EQ into notice. I highly recommend *Biblical EQ* by John Edmiston if you want to know more about how to use Scripture to stabilize and mature emotions.

DEALING WITH RESENTMENTS

Resentment is the most dominant emotional response that sabotages recovery. The AA *Big Book* calls it "the number one offender." I used to remind the men, "Don't get bitter. Get better." The only way to get over resentment is to forgive the offender, yourself, and sometimes even God! We touched on this in Chapter 9, The Miracle of AA, but it is worth repeating.

Forgiveness is the foundational doctrine of Christianity; therefore, it is also a foundational principle of AA and every good recovery program. Resentment is the opposite of forgiveness. When you harbor resentment, you either refuse to forgive others or yourself. And as I said before, sometimes you even resent what you believe God has allowed to happen to you, so you resent Him.

Forgiving God is something every person who was abused and traumatically hurt as a child must come to terms with. When we come to see the nature and character of God, we know He did everything He could to protect us. His love for us gives us the ability to "forgive" Him because He was not the abuser or the cause of our trauma. God gives unconditional love, salvation, and healing.

In recovery, we see God's hand in others forgiving us for our faults, failures, and mistakes. We feel grateful, which fuels recovery. If we relapse, they forgive us again and help us get back into recovery. Our gratitude grows. Forgiveness is a catalyst for gratitude and purges the heart of resentment and bitterness. Forgiveness and gratitude work together to get us sober and keep us sober. To recover our lives, we must learn to handle resentment by learning to forgive and asking others to forgive us. Eventually, we will move completely away from resentment, never allowing it to capture our thoughts and emotions. Emotional maturity cultivates a forgiving attitude and lifestyle.

This new lifestyle and attitude of forgiveness usually doesn't happen overnight. Often, even the strongest of us find ourselves nursing an offense, poking old wounds to keep them festering with bitterness. At such times, we must remember: There are no small resentments! Every resentment is like a dose of poison, and the more poison you take in, the more you are prone to relapse and eventually die.

The devil uses resentment to encourage and justify a relapse. That's why resentment is everywhere in the world—society markets resentment. Our top-rated TV shows and movies are about resentment and a thirst for revenge on the bad guys. The media encourages us to think this way, making us angry victims who are not treated fairly and don't get what we feel we deserve. Everyone in recovery must learn how to throw out their resentments and become a forgiver. We can't battle resentments with intellect because the smarter we are, the better we justify our bitter thoughts and feelings. How do we combat resentment and reach a place of forgiveness?

First, we have to recognize our resentments, which the 12 Steps of AA specifically facilitates.

We need God's help because sometimes we don't recognize our resentments, and He must reveal them to us. We also need His help to see what part we have played in the resentment. God helps us distinguish the truth from our justifications.

Unless asking someone to forgive us will cause them harm, asking someone to forgive us for our wrongdoing is vital to us forgiving ourselves. A good counselor will say, "Even if they don't forgive you, you can live in the knowledge that you have done the right thing—and can forgive them for not forgiving you! Then you can forgive yourself for your wrongdoing." This experience gets us off the condemnation and shame treadmill that causes relapse. We begin to forgive ourselves, which is critical. If we cannot forgive ourselves, resentments will remain, and we will likely relapse.

Step 10 is the maintenance step to keep resentment out of our lives for good. Living like this turns us into a person who quickly forgives, knowing that forgiving keeps us not only sober but peaceful and content. It also keeps us from hurting others and having to make more amends!

Both forgiving and asking to be forgiven are hard work. Knowing this, the disciples asked Jesus about forgiveness.

Then Peter came to Him and said, "Lord, how often shall my brother sin against me, and I forgive him? Up to seven times?" Jesus said to him, "I do not say to you, up to seven times, but up to seventy times seven.

Matthew 18:21–22

Peter must have been shocked at the prospect of having to forgive someone for committing the same offense against him seventy times seven, but Jesus made it clear that this was vitally important. Clearly, Jesus was saying to forgive often and quickly. He knows it's hard to be grateful when we are filled with resentments, but gratitude comes naturally when we forgive others.

Both clinical and especially Christian programs should model forgiveness. Punitive measures often demonstrate resentment and condemnation. The recovering person sees them as not walking the talk. It's hard to help a person develop new attitudes and behavior without modeling them ourselves. We all must become supernatural forgivers—lean, fine-tuned gratitude athletes with zero resentment fat. A good gratitude athlete will have forgiving power over resentments and dispatch them when they try to creep into their life. I'm a gratitude athlete, and my gratitude coach is Jesus. (He's still taking on coaching jobs, just in case you are looking for one!)

COMPONENTS OF EQ

Secular EQ has developed a list of six components of emotional maturity. People in recovery need teaching and coaching in all of them.

1. Self-awareness

2. Self-regulation

3. Empathy

4. Interpersonal Relationships

5. Social Responsibility

6. Stress Management

1. Self-awareness. While drinking or using drugs, we deceive ourselves about ourselves. We have little-to-no self-awareness.

2. Self-regulation. When practicing our addiction, it is impossible to regulate ourselves if there is no carrot at the end of the stick (drugs, alcohol).

3. Empathy. We can go ballistic over the smallest things that disturb us, but we are emotionally unavailable when others need an emotional response from us. Our genuine emotions feel awkward and are often frightening, so we avoid them or fake them. Without a carrot at the end of the stick, we avoid situations that require emotional responses.

3. Empathy and 4. Interpersonal Relationship are obviously connected.

4. Interpersonal Relationship and 5. Social Responsibility are difficult for the same reason: Addicts are emotionally immature.

What cripples the addict most is their inability to have a healthy relationship. All our relationships have been governed by the carrot at the end of the stick: obtaining a fix. We become like Pavlov's dog and less human. Drugs and alcohol impair our ability to understand and control our self-centeredness. It's been noted that we start in the crowd but end up alone. We are total recluses except when we need something. We must learn to conduct a right, healthy relationship.

Some secular methods use plants or pets as a means to teach about relationships. If you can keep a plant or a pet alive for a year, you are ready for a relationship with a human. Plant or pet therapy approaches relationship problems with basic tasks needed to sustain life in the relationship. It's used with married couples, recluse folks, addicts, and prisoners. It's a simple remedy, especially with plants, which are low risk. Pets, however, are a higher risk. They are socially interactive and require more care. If a plant dies because you forget to water it, you replace it and hopefully do better. If your dog dies because you forgot to water and feed it, a living being has lost its life because of your negligence. This can be devastating and lead to relapse.

Biblical emotional healing addresses relationships from a spiritual perspective. The foundation of all good relationships begin and are monitored through the right relationship with a loving God. With His help, we can intuitively know how to have the right relationship with other people.

6. Stress Management is a beast for those finding their way emotionally, as there are many known and unknown stressors. The sources of stress can be gender struggles, ethnicity struggles, sexual urges, bullying, cultural and subcultural issues, economic status, and relationships such as marriage, motherhood, or fatherhood. Being aware of stressors and having plans to navigate them is very important in any counseling. Unconscious, unresolved emotions just waiting under the surface could destroy plans in seconds during a particularly stressful time.

Counselors and mentors must address these six components for the client to become emotionally mature and stabilize their emotions.

STABILIZATION

A basic but critical skill in developing emotional maturity is stabilization. Because memories, thoughts, and emotions affect judgment, an addict is always on the brink of bad behavior and relapse. A good counselor will put the addict through stabilization exercises that train them to identify the emotion, deal with it, and avoid destructive behavior and relapse. Some counselors encourage addicts to separate themselves from the emotion, but because I know how hard it was to separate myself from something that was me, I don't usually dwell too much on this step. The important thing is to identify the emotion so it can be dealt with.

I usually suggest that the client own the emotion (I'm angry, I'm sad, I'm depressed). Then I suggest ways to regulate the emotion, teaching them that all feelings are temporary and subject to them. I ask what the emotion is doing to them, and to describe their feelings and thoughts. The more cognitive you can make the emotion, the more chance they have to regulate it. Addicts can sometimes accomplish this with a good friend who will sit with them and cry with them. Healing comes by facing emotions dead on and moving through them with a wise and caring counselor or friend.

Laughter is another stabilizing tool. Addicts often engage in dark humor during AA meetings, but laughing to keep from crying is more than just an old saying! It is a way to stabilize their emotions to have the strength to go through the healing process. Laughing is a temporary fix, but over time it takes the sting out of emotions caused by a traumatic past. And hearing others laugh promotes healing. Seeing that others have experienced what they have experienced, yet laughing about it, gives the addict hope and stability to face their own demons.

Exercise and fresh air are great ways to level and stabilize emotions. I used my work of cleaning floors and bathrooms in this way, often meditating on Scripture as I worked. I would always encourage biblical meditation, as the only spirit you want to help you is God's Holy Spirit! Meditation in the Word of God has been my strongest asset in my emotional battles. I take stories in the Bible and put them in my own words. In this way, the Word of God does what it always does: gives me peace and new understanding.

Praying to God is stabilizing. I pray to my Heavenly Father, avoiding recited prayers and engaging in conversational, open, and honest prayers. I anticipate answers from Him, knowing He counts on me to be patient and wait for His answer. His answer comes in many different ways: in His still, small voice, by a sign, or through a verse, a friend, or a stranger.

Memorizing Scripture is another way to stabilize emotions. Memorization takes discipline and can also be a team effort.

The telephone is another powerful tool in emotional stabilization, although it is a hard discipline to master. In the rooms of AA, we jokingly call it "the 100-pound phone" because it's so hard to pick up when we need to phone a friend for help.

The addict may think they don't need to practice stabilization, but at any moment, their life may depend on being able to stabilize themselves rapidly. It may seem corny, but practicing stabilization with a counselor and then with a support group can save their life one day. I can't say this strongly enough: Practicing stabilization is critical and helpful not only for the addict but also for their support team. With practice, the team won't be caught by surprise, nor will its members. They will be ready to spring into action when needed.

These stabilization techniques encourage transparency and identify relapse warning signs. Teaching them to friends and family allows them to help the addict (and do better themselves) to manage warning signs and maintain emotional stability. The addict will get so good at transparency that they will be helpful to everyone around them. People will benefit from what they bring to the table, and their recovery can be a blessing to their family and community.

A Safe Place to Learn

As director of the recovery program in San Jose, I put on big events called Family Day to provide a safe environment for clients to work on emotional stability and maturity. The men would invite their families for food, games, and family fellowship. All my case managers would attend, moving around, engaging in conversation, and observing the different family dynamics.

For some clients, it was the first time in a long time they had relaxed over a meal, played a game together, or carried on a conversation with their spouse or family. On special holidays, we would get gifts for the dads to give their children and take family photos, which we printed for the family to take home. There's something about family photos that brings about unity and encourages unconditional love and forgiveness.

One Christmas, my client Roger met his son Billy for the first time. Roger had been in prison for a drug offense when Billy was born. The prison was far away, and his family was poor so they never visited him. His son Billy was five years old, and his mother, Rose, was coaxing little Billy to go to his father. Billy would not go. Roger turned to me, and I took him into my office. He broke down and wept uncontrollably. I knew Roger was in a dark place emotionally. I thanked God this had happened in a safe environment, where he could work through this and not throw in the towel.

Roger sobbed, "Mr. Knuckles, my son doesn't even recognize me. He's scared of me." I sat and listened as he cursed himself for being a mess-up and terrible dad. I gave him time to grieve, but then I reminded him: He was still Billy's father, and Billy would come to know that. He just had to take it slow. Be patient. I did not put pressure on him to become an instant super-dad or super-husband. I just reminded him that relationships take time. I understood he was at the precipice of chucking it all away, relapse, because I had experienced this too.

"Right now, Roger, could you settle for a smile from your son?" I remembered this bizarre quote I once heard from Bishop Desmond Tutu, "How do you eat an elephant? One bite at a time." I took Roger over to the kids' games and told him we were going to watch his son throw a ball. "I bet you can help Billy learn to throw," I told him.

I watched as Roger, Rose, and Billy played game after game, and then the magic moment happened. Billy called out to Roger, "Look at this, Daddy!" Roger smiled bigger than I ever saw him smile before. He had taken baby steps, and he learned that he didn't have to relapse at an emotionally overloaded moment. He saw that a bad moment didn't have to last and could soon pass. Family Day was doing what it was supposed to do: bring about emotional healing for the client and his family members.

HEALING CRY

When the Christian rehab program director took a few of us in recovery to a National Day of Prayer Breakfast, I had never seen such an event. I marveled at all the people there. I walked away from the group for a moment, and a man asked me how I came to be there. I told him my story of homelessness, addiction, and how I got saved. Halfway through my story, he started to cry. He was a huge, strong man—and he was crying!

I marveled at this man's tears for me. Then he wrote out a large check for the mission, which I gave to our director. I could not get the tears of this godly man out of my mind. I had not cried in years. Even when I gave my life to Christ, I was filled with emotion but remained tearless. I thought something was wrong with me. This wasn't the first Christian man I had seen cry, and I wanted to cry too. That night in my prayers, I asked God for the ability to cry. I wanted tears of my own.

By this time, I had met Jack, who also was a massive man. I'm six feet tall, and he towered over me. He could bench press well over 300 pounds almost effortlessly. I hung out with Jack a lot when I was in the recovery program. He volunteered at the mission, and we spent a lot of time in the truck making runs for food. One day, he asked me to go with him to high schools to speak about the dangers of addiction. I was excited at the idea of sharing my story and agreed.

The day after the prayer breakfast and my prayer to God to cry again, I went with Jack to speak at a large high school. I got up on stage to deliver my talk, which I had given several times before. I opened my mouth and got as far as, "Hi everybody. I'm Charles." The tears came flowing down. I was crying so hard; my gut was heaving. I can't imagine what the kids thought. I had no idea God would answer my prayers so quickly—and publicly!

Jack walked up on the stage and hugged me. He cradled my head in his massive hands, pressed my head against his huge chest, and said, "Let it all out, man." And I did!

After a while, I slipped my head out of his hand and whispered, "I can't breathe, Jack." I was crying that hard. Somehow, I managed to give my talk, and the kids and staff deeply appreciated it.

That day God broke the dam of my pent-up emotions, and Jack gave me permission to release them. It was real, I had no control, and I loved how the Holy Spirit freed me from so much grief and sadness—and gave me joy. I've been able to cry ever since! I am no longer awkward or look down on men who are secure enough to cry. To me, it is a gift from God that heals us.

God not only wants us to be sober and free from our addictions; He wants to make us whole, to give us joy, to bring us good, healthy relationships. The fight for emotional maturity is a long, hard road for anyone with any kind of addiction, but it is well worth the fight! When we begin to experience emotional stability, a huge part of our recovery becomes productive and fulfilling for us and everyone in our lives.

GOD NOT ONLY WANTS US TO BE SOBER AND FREE FROM OUR ADDICTIONS; HE WANTS TO MAKE US WHOLE, TO GIVE US JOY, TO BRING US GOOD, HEALTHY RELATIONSHIPS.

APPLICATIONS

CHAPTER FOURTEEN

A COMPLETE RECOVERY PROGRAM

Addiction is generally defined as a physical, psychological, and social disease in the secular clinical world. However, in Christian clinical circles, we are aware of a fourth area—the spiritual element. The challenge I've encountered with Christian clinicians is that they claim the spiritual aspect is so important, they neglect or even deny the importance of the physical, psychological, and social elements. On the other hand, secular clinicians will admit the spiritual aspect but take it a step further and say, "It's spiritual, not religious." In this way, they accept anything as being spiritual and condemn organized religion. I have come to believe differently.

I believe the Bible teaches that all four elements are essential, and we should have recovery plans to support each element. The clinical community covers the first three somewhat thoroughly but is random about the fourth, often discouraging participating in church. On the other hand, the Christian community is very specific on the spiritual component but basically leaves the other three as suggestions. I attempt to bring these two communities together, giving a complete solution for the client. I have already spent an entire chapter on the spiritual element, so let's take a good look at the other three elements.

The Physical Element

When we talk about the physical element of addiction, what comes to mind are diet and exercise. These things are important, but there is more to it. Watch how addicts move and express themselves. They may lower their head around people they consider normal and of more value than themselves. They might have a nervous tic or stutter. The Bible calls this the wages of sin (Romans 6:23). For years, addicts have lied, stolen, and lived for themselves. They have hurt others to get what they want. Their sins weigh them down mentally, emotionally, and physically. Over time, their face and body tell the story of their lifestyle. Bent over. Unable to speak clearly—completely wasted physically.

Dishonesty, cowardice, guilt, and shame draw lines in the face and develop expressions in body language that become permanent. The organs in the body begin to weaken, and immunity fades. Sinning puts them in the fight-or-flight mode. This is manageable for short periods of time, but being in this mode for long periods of time takes its toll on the body. The immune system breaks down, the nervous system goes haywire, bones become weaker, and even chromosomes are affected. The Bible is right: Sin breaks down the physical body and, if not stopped, sin will kill you.

Most believe that the physical self, according to the extent of damage, is the least complicated to understand. It is, therefore, the first step in recovery. However, the physical damage can be very complicated as some damage cannot be seen by the naked eye. Therefore physicians must be involved with complete recoveries. We first judge the extent of damage in a person by how they look. This is not right or wrong; it is simply not *all there is*. It is the first resource available in assessing the client, but we must have them undergo a complete physical examination.

After we know exactly what physical issues the client is dealing with, certain medications may be necessary. If possible, we should also enlist the services of a nutritionist and a physical trainer, being careful to follow the physician's advice. As the client follows the diet prescribed by their physician/nutritionist and practices the exercises prescribed by their trainer, they will become stronger and more confident every day. Just developing the self-discipline to heal and strengthen their body gives them a new hope that they are capable of doing what is right and say no to what is wrong.

With this point, we see how all the elements of recovery intersect. Dealing with physical issues affects psychological and social issues. Feeling healthy and physically sound builds confidence in oneself and in others. And overall, most clients realize that without the help of God, they cannot persevere in the routines of self-discipline that are needed to recover physically, psychologically, and socially.

THE PSYCHOLOGICAL ELEMENT

Deeply affecting the physical body are the cognitive or mental responses like guilt, shame, and the "what if I get found out" scenarios that endlessly loop in the client's brain. Beyond our primary addiction, we have acquired many less apparent addictions. These addictions are both psychological and physical. We may use caffeine, sugar, and nicotine to excess. Our habits of thinking drive us to them, and they chemically reinforce our thinking to crave them. It is a vicious cycle.

There are chemical responses in your brain and body. The biochemical onslaught chips away at the immune system, opening the way to cancer, infection, and disease. Hormones unleashed by stress eat at the digestive tract and lungs, promoting ulcers and asthma—or they may weaken the heart, leading to strokes and heart disease. There are signals from hormones that stimulate glands to release other hormones that could be considered killers.

In studies of the amygdala, it has been found that this part of the brain is sensitive to the history or pattern of dishonest behavior. The studies support what they call a "slippery slope," in that what might begin as a small act of dishonesty can escalate into more significant acts of dishonesty. The brain chemically adapts to dishonesty or sin.

In essence, one sin creates another sin. We literally sear our conscience from being able to feel guilt and conviction when we lie.

Physical recovery pushes through to aid the psychological recovery. As we become healthier physically, our brains function better. We can see more clearly to address psychological or mental damage. Some of the drug-induced psychoses will subside. Just about all drugs have their own set of induced psychoses, even prescription drugs. According to the National Institute of Mental Health, all mood-altering substances can induce psychoses that mimic schizophrenia.

The recovering alcoholic or addict who has not incurred permanent brain damage will start to recover. Nervous system damage can take up to 24 months to recover to normal, near-normal, or manageable. Most recovery programs are 28 days, 90 days, or one year. Some clients can become functional in 28 days, some in 90 days, but most need at least a year or two in a structured, grace-driven rehab to become a functioning, healthy person.

With all the abuse to my body, I had a hard time learning. I had to learn how to learn! Figuring out how to retain information is one of the many challenges that helped me to understand the addict mind so well. I was able to develop classes that employed the process needed for addicted brains to retain information. This was key to avoiding relapse and staying sober.

Clinicians used to think that co-occurring mental health issues and addiction were not that common, but now most agree that they are. The problem with this revelation is that legally, the mental health piece of recovery needs to be addressed by a psychologist alone, but the psychologist should be conferring with the addict's addiction counselor and physician as well. If the psychologist is not a Christian, they may be completely unaware of the client's spiritual maladies and, without knowing it, steer the client away from the very things they need. Again, a good recovery program includes all four elements.

When faced with undiagnosed mental health issues, religious communities need to enlist the help of a caring Christian psychologist or licensed addiction therapist. Prayer, worship, and good sermons are beneficial, but sometimes healing requires more than these. Prayer for and by the addict should be for God to reveal their path of recovery.

He knows what they need, and sometimes He may point them to a psychologist who specializes in addiction.

On the other hand, most secular clinics see no value in prayer, worship, Scripture reading, or a church community. They just don't recognize the need to work together. Unfortunately, people in need fall through these large cracks due to money as much as a lack of understanding. More specialists mean more money, and those without the money are left out. Without a church community to see that they get what they need, the addict continues in their nightmare of a life.

The mental health piece may be more complicated and involve more work. It depends on the client. Some have difficulty facing physical problems; others have a hard time admitting they have any mental or emotional issues. I find that most clients have difficulty with the psychological piece because they have been told (and their demons have told them) they are crazy and have acted weird their whole lives. It is essential to get them to see that they have choices where their thinking, emotions, and behavior are concerned.

Again, the spiritual element is crucial in dealing with psychological issues. As Christians, we know God has given us "the mind of Christ" (1 Corinthians 2:16). With physical, psychological, and social issues, we have a miracle-working God who loves us and wants the best for us. This encourages the client and gives them hope. They see a light at the end of an often very dark tunnel, knowing that as they do the work and trust in God, He will heal their mind and body.

THE SOCIAL ELEMENT

As we have discussed, addicts are unable to have the right relationships. Recovering clients must learn how to have good, healthy relationships in their support groups, the rooms of AA, with their counselors and friends, and with their church community. The first places I felt accepted were in the rooms of AA and my church. In AA, we were all addicts with a terrible story to tell, so I knew I belonged. On the other hand, my church was composed of people who, on the surface, had absolutely nothing in common with me. They were white, and I was black; they were successful, and I was a custodian; they lived in wealthy neighborhoods, and I rented a studio apartment by a busy highway; they were highly educated, and I was educated in the streets. We were poles apart, so why did it work so well? We realized that the grace of God was working in all of us, regardless of our background. Many of their struggles were not like mine, but they still had struggles, and Jesus was the answer to all of them.

Recovery is not a solo ride because life is not a solo ride. God created us to be social creatures, and we are at our best when we need each other. Unfortunately, most addicts push people away and shut them out for various reasons. I pushed my son Carlos away when I was in deep distress. Later, when I was helping other men become better fathers and husbands, I was filled with sorrow over my own estrangement from my son. I had not seen Carlos for years and didn't know where to look for him. I finally found him through a friend.

When we met, it was painful, but I saw that he had grown to be a strong and handsome man, with five sons and two daughters. I discovered that I had amazingly talented grandchildren! I love spending time with them and go to their sports events when I can. One granddaughter is a singer and acts in middle-school plays. I try not to spoil them when they come to visit, but I can't help myself. I missed so much time with their dad that I guess I'm trying to make up for it. This would never have happened without God's saving grace and all those who supported me in recovery.

Addicts punish themselves in isolation because of disappointments and hurt from their past. Sometimes, they do foolish things to get back at or get the attention of people who have hurt them. Rarely are they sociopaths; they don't want to hurt anyone but themselves. They're in pain, so they hide. They need someone to find them and refuse to leave until they come out of the shadows.

When you see someone in trouble, with visible signs of distress, what you see is a human implosion. The outward signs of homelessness and addiction are inward cries for help. If a human among other humans is crying out, you are called to help, especially as a believer in Jesus

RECOVERY IS NOT A SOLO RIDE BECAUSE LIFE IS NOT A SOLO RIDE. GOD CREATED US TO BE SOCIAL CREATURES, AND WE ARE AT OUR BEST WHEN WE NEED EACH OTHER.

Christ. Compassion is your response. If you feel nothing, you need help! However, I also caution you to not put yourself in danger. Work with a reputable charity or your church. Don't give out any information about yourself to strangers or open your wallet to give a person on the street a couple of dollars. There are smart ways to help, and the Bible reminds us to use wisdom.

I was very social when I first began using drugs and alcohol. I even had a serious girlfriend. But eventually, addiction and all of its damage separated me from having the right relationships with anyone, even my girlfriend. Sin is the spiritual sickness that leads to all other abnormalities, including addictions and an inability to have a healthy relationship. People who aren't addicts are either conned into maintaining a pseudo-relationship with us or soon realize they have no common ground. The bottom line becomes clear: They are pursuing life, and we are pursuing death.

Being alone is the social conundrum of addicts. It is like being in the eye of the hurricane: All is quiet, but we are generating chaos and destruction all around us. We don't know we are in the storm, much less how to get out of it. The social element begins to heal the moment someone begins to pray for and minister to us. This is the surprise of grace that shocks the addict into wonder. They wonder how this person could care. They wonder why the person cares. I have no doubt that the Christian woman in the store I tried to rob prayed for me, that she had her friends and church pray for me, and God answered their prayers. I know that because I do whenever I meet someone who is caught in addiction.

Being surprised by grace time and again happens in a social context. You receive grace when you walk into rehab, when you sit with a counselor, when you meet with your support group and go to AA meetings, and as you become a member of a church community. Being surprised by grace, you find it easier and easier to give grace to others. You forgive. You even begin to forgive yourself. You have compassion. You are not so quick to judge, to be jealous, or to be offended. Over time, you enjoy the miracle of close, genuine relationships based on honesty and truth. All of this happens because someone began to pray, someone surprised you with God's grace.

Relationships are healthy to the extent that we have a healthy relationship with God. Our relationship with Him must be first, and then all other relationships fall into line. Our social life in Jesus Christ slowly dispels the hurricane that has held us in a lonely place of isolation, and we step into the sunshine with new hope and joy. Instead of fearing people and trying to get something we want from them, we actually begin to enjoy our family, our friends, and our fellow addicts—and we want to be a blessing to them.

THE SPIRITUAL ELEMENT REVISITED

I love my AA group, but sometimes they get frustrated with me for talking about Jesus. Once, I got frustrated, stood up, and said, "Where were you when I stood on that chair and put a rope around my neck to kill the pain? You were probably in an AA meeting, but Jesus was there, and He saved me. Not you, but Jesus. So, He's my Higher Power." As a result, several people in that meeting came to have a personal relationship with Him. The others grew to respect His power that was clearly working in my life.

Jesus referred to himself as a seed that had to die and be planted in the ground, because then a new creation would sprout and grow to produce a multitude of seeds just like Him. The addict learns that their whole life has revolved around them. They are their own god and the center of their world. When they are repeatedly surprised by the grace of God, they see Him in those who offer them His grace. Then, one day, they make the decision to let Him be their God and call the shots in their life. Ironically, by dying to themselves, they are made alive to God. It is a miracle the natural mind cannot fathom, but we fully know and accept this reality as a new, born-again spirit.

Religiously, we think if the client can just know God, they will get better. We pray over them to show them how to pray, even if they are unfamiliar with the language of prayer. We may have them say the famous

"Sinner's Prayer" and tell them they are saved. Of course, all we've really done (in good faith) is go through a ritual that may mean nothing to the addict, who is also very fragile. We also may unintentionally turn them off from pursuing God. We must remember that only the Holy Spirit can convict a person that they are a sinner in need of a savior, and that savior is Jesus. We cannot talk anyone into it. Our responsibility is to share the Gospel; then it is between them and the Holy Spirit.

The addict also may not be well enough in body and mind to understand what we are saying. They cannot relate to God or us in any healthy social way. The very idea of a loving Heavenly Father, sending His Son to die for their sins in order to forgive them, is too much for them to process. After all, just the mention of "father" could mean only pain and suffering to them. Yes, God can break through their confusion, but if He chooses not to, we must continue to model His grace, faithfulness, and understanding. Again, we must be consistent in our walk and never forceful in our talk. After years of not believing most of what they hear, addicts are visual learners. Seeing is believing!

We must not neglect any of the four elements of recovery. Physical healing is usually the first step, which helps to heal the mind. And once the client is healthy physically and mentally, they begin to build a healthy emotional and social life. We introduce the spiritual life all along the way, mostly through our attitudes and actions. We encourage them to become an active member of a church that will disciple them in faith and nurture their relationship with God and others.

With all these elements working in a client's life, they stand the best chance of emerging from the darkness of addiction and sustaining a life of freedom in the light. This is what I call a complete recovery program.

CHAPTER FIFTEEN

TOOLS FOR RECOVERY — TOOLS FOR LIFE

I've served in recovery for over 20 years. For 12 of those years in San Jose, I was director of a 72-bed rehab and oversaw a 60-bed homeless shelter for men. We also served over 300 meals per day to the homeless and hungry. I supervised all three programs at the same time, improving them by increasing their capacity and efficiency.

In this part of the book, I take joy in sharing what I've learned as both a person who desperately needed help to recover and a person who has helped hundreds of people recover—from jail to Yale. My prayer is that counselors, volunteers, coaches, mentors, and even family members of those in recovery will gain some wisdom and valuable tools to use.

The following tools are essential for alcoholics and addicts to recover and make new lives for themselves. To be honest, they are all based on the Bible. God knows what works and what doesn't! Consequently, the same tools and principles are essential for any Christian to live a full life. With confidence, I can say that whether you are recovering, helping someone else recover, or want a better life, these tools will help you. They are really tools for all of us, whatever we are going through.

TOOL #1: RECOVERY IS INDIVIDUAL

My path of recovery is unique, but so is every other person's. It's a mystery that some people can get sober without a counselor or Alcoholics Anonymous meetings. Some people just go to church and fully rely on God. Some have the inner fortitude to recognize their addiction, "just say no," and quit forever. Others lean on family and friends and are able to maintain sobriety. Most people, however, need a lot of guidance and encouragement through rehab, counseling, and AA meetings.

In my early recovery, I attended about three AA meetings a week. Even though I was mainly a drug addict, I found the AA meetings more spiritual. Also, I went to church on Sundays and got involved with church activities during the week. I did a lot of volunteering at a Christian mission as well. My recovery was based in my Christian faith. "The God of my understanding" was the God of the Bible, whom I know through Jesus Christ and recognize as the one, true God and Creator of the Universe.

My calling is to help addicts and alcoholics get sober and stay sober by recognizing they are spiritual beings with a spiritual Father who loves them and wants them whole. I am not called by God to present a path to recovery without Him. However, when some reject the Christian view and choose another god, I still do my best to help them. I privately pray for them to know Jesus, but again, everyone's recovery is unique, and some cannot fathom God's grace without sobriety.

Because of my desire to help others recover from their addictions, I became a counselor. The knowledge I gained with the certifications and licenses in counseling helped me in recovery too. As I have said, the first thing I recognized was that everyone does recovery differently, that what works for me may not work for someone else. The key is to find what works! Involving the client as much as possible, we figure out a plan of recovery that is suited for them.

TOOL #2: CLIENT-CENTERED THERAPY

The client-centered therapeutic approach simply gives the client ownership of their recovery plan. It is driven by their input and decisions. I like this method because it's more about the client than the counselor. Instead of dictating to them what they need to do, we first get information from them. What is most important to them? What are their plans? Where do they want to go from here? How can their recovery plan fit into a career path or improve their family situation? Together, the counselor and client agree on what needs to change and how to make those changes happen. With ownership of their recovery plan, the client is more invested in the process. Recovery becomes their idea and not something forced upon them.

I had a client (we'll just call him Q) who was a neo-Nazi. I knew that the client-centered approach would be the key to any success for him. He came to me straight out of prison, where he was a member of a white supremacist gang. His anger and resentment were a source of survival for him. In addition, he was addicted primarily to alcohol, but several other things as well. At the core of all these maladies was his hate for black people. When he looked up and saw a black man as his counselor at our first meeting, we both knew this was going to be interesting!

Q was a huge man who towered over everyone. He was a leader, and I knew I had to get him into a leadership role in his treatment plan. By letting him know he was in charge of many of the choices presented in his recovery process, I also told him that he was the central actor in his recovery. I was subtle in my approach to guide him in his own treatment plan.

Thankfully, Q confessed he thought he had failed at recovery in the past because he did not give God a chance. We eventually found common ground in his interest in becoming more spiritual. In the group,

I would purposely give Q a little more time to respond to spiritual ideas. He started researching and preparing for his times to share in the group and was among those who took notes.

I always encourage a discovery process. I've found that information is more valuable if the client discovers it rather than someone lecturing them. Q began to thrive in his process. He had not known that he was capable of what he was now doing. When he was ready to confess the atrocities he had committed on people of color, he chose me as his confessor! In this way, he was surprised by his own accomplishments.

One week in November, I took ten of my clients along with fifteen clients from other facilities to Death Valley for camping and hiking. The trip was sponsored and led by some seasoned church volunteers. Q was among the eager clients. We had a long drive from San Jose to a very remote area in Death Valley. The volunteer leader had led dozens of trips like this and knew his way around. However, as an urban guy, I was lost! I was completely dependent on our leader.

We walked through a rainbow-colored canyon, where the pathways were lined by huge canyon walls. It was almost dizzying. I fell way behind the group, and although I was a bit concerned about being lost, I tried not to show it. Q held back and stayed by my side. I felt guilty because I knew he could keep up with the others. I said, "Don't worry about me. Go have fun with the guys. I'll catch up."

I'll never forget the expression on his face as he said, "No, Mr. Knuckles. I'm right where I'm supposed to be. I like chatting with you." We had a great few days together. Then we stopped at a place with a pool. I was so touched when Q said, "There's some water. Will you baptize me here?"

As I prepared to dip him in the water, I taught him the tradition of baptism. He would be immersed in Jesus' death as he went down in the water, dying to all sin, then he would be resurrected with Jesus into a new life in Him as he came out of the water. Suddenly, I was worried about his massive size. Would I be able to dip him and lift him? I lowered Q, with all his Nazi tattoos, into the pool. Cradled in my arms, I felt him go limp and totally surrender to God. Somehow, I was able to lift him up, and we both felt tremendous gratitude to God!

TOOL #3: GRATITUDE

Gratitude and thanksgiving are talked about a lot in the Bible, because God knows how the world can bring a person down. God is all about lifting people up, and so He encourages us to be thankful, to find something to be grateful for every day—and sometimes every moment of the day. With a heart of gratitude, the world cannot bring you down, and it's a lot easier to stay sober when you're lifted up.

Not only does gratitude change you, but it is contagious. Coming from a leader like Q, gratitude became contagious to the clients around him. This is the power of gratitude: His gratitude ran so deep, it served as a healing balm to his wife, his son, and his family, as well as to almost any person who crossed his path. His gratitude not only continues to heal him, but it replicates more gratitude in others.

You can read about the power of gratitude in both the Bible and the *Big Book* of Alcoholics Anonymous. Being thankful may seem too simple, but like all simple, biblical principles, it is powerful. Being thankful carries the grace of God to transform a person and is one of the most dynamic elements in recovery.

You might ask, "How do I get to gratitude if resentment is my default?" Gratitude has to be intentional. Like any new habit, establishing gratitude as your default takes time and practice. You learn to recognize resentment when it surfaces and find something to be grateful for despite it. When nothing seems to be going your way, or you find yourself in a huge mess of your own making, it's upsetting and easy to be bitter.

Resentment fuels relapse, but gratitude fuels recovery.

You must see resentment as your enemy! Think of stories that illustrate gratitude or someone in your life who models gratitude. Go to someone who can help you list reasons to thank God. Very few people discover and maintain gratitude on their own. Usually, there is some divine intervention, and there are as many different interventions as there are people. One might not realize they are in an intervention until later when they look back on their life—and are grateful.

My intervention that inspired gratitude was a hug and, "We've been waiting for you." God supernaturally enabled me to go through detox and stop smoking, and then my church family freely gave me what I needed most, when I needed it and without hesitation. Q experienced gratitude when he found the most unlikely friend and counselor in me, a black man. Jesus healed him of his hatred toward black people and gave him a new nature of caring for others as he cared for me on the camping trip. Gratitude springs from experiencing love and grace from God through others—sometimes in the most unlikely divine intervention.

Gratitude is often a steep learning curve, especially if wounds of the past are deep. For the severely wounded, resentments and anger are strong, but the miraculous healing of a wound can be the intervention that inspires them to be grateful. It's nearly impossible for resentment to coexist with genuine gratitude, especially when God's love and grace have restored and healed you.

How do we get to a place of absolute gratitude, free from resentment? We must first accept the fact that this is a constant battle. A friend told me, "It's one thing to be in a war, but it's another to be in a war and not know it." We must accept that we have to guard our hearts against harboring resentment and turn our thoughts to what we are grateful for. No matter how free we get, people will disappoint us, make us angry, and even betray us. We have to forgive, turn them over to God, and think of all the good things He has done, is doing, and can do in our lives and theirs.

Christian teachers call this the battle in your mind, of your mind, and for your mind. What you choose to think about and how you choose to think about it makes the difference between gratitude and resentment, recovery and relapse. And it's something you do daily. Regardless of your difficulties, despite your setbacks, you're in the fight every day of your life and recovery.

I still nurse little resentments now and then, but I am able to catch myself, pray for strength and guidance, and discuss them with other believers. This enables me to keep my feet firmly planted in gratitude. I fight to stay cognitive of the fact that resentments have no value. They are destructive and can only harm me. Not so with gratitude. Many psychologists and scientists have agreed that there is a high value to gratitude. There are endless studies showing how gratitude boosts happiness, alleviates some forms of depression, is good for your health, and shifts your thinking from negative to positive. In fact, gratitude elicits surges of "feel good" hormones like dopamine, serotonin, and oxytocin!

Oxytocin is a hormone that's sometimes known as the "cuddle hormone" or the "love hormone" because it is released when people snuggle up or bond with one another. In other words, gratitude is like getting a big hug from a relative or close friend. I like to think of gratitude as a bond that brings me closer to God as I become the person He created me to be.

Seriously, I would like you to consider being able to snuggle with your Heavenly Father. When no one else is around, go to the end of your sofa, take a pillow or two and a warm comforter, and snuggle into the arm of the sofa. Cover yourself with the comforter and hug the pillow. Then have a conversation with your Father God. Run through your recent successes, opportunities missed, and things you could have done better. As you talk to Him about your decisions and the situations you face, listen to Him. Give Him some time to speak to you, comfort you, and counsel you. Thank Him, tell Him you love Him and why. Your heart will fill with gratitude!

However you do it, find the time to be alone with God with no distractions at least twice a week, every day if possible. I would like you to feel overwhelmed by His love to such an extent that hormones you can't see are released to comfort you. God's healing powers are free and available to everyone! And they are so much better than expensive medicines that might not always be available.

Gratitude is an organic health food! It has only positive effects and fuels recovery from any wound or trauma you have experienced.

Decide to be grateful. Make it your state of mind. Be stubborn about being grateful! Insist on being grateful. Once you know the value of gratitude, once you experience it, you will fight for it. Even in overwhelming pressure to be resentful, remember its value and fight to be thankful.

When I think I can't be grateful for anything in my present trouble, all I have to do is look at the Cross, and I'm overwhelmed with gratitude. I'm literally stunned at God's love for me, at Jesus' sacrifice for me. I remember that when I am weak, He is strong in me (2 Corinthians 12:10). The Holy Spirit in me is the same power that raised Jesus from the dead (Romans 8:11). And I can do all things through Him who strengthens me (Philippians 4:13)!

Gratitude hit me hard, and I'm glad it did. I pray you will know the value of being grateful for all of God's blessings and the people He sends to help you, that you will make it a daily habit to defeat any resentment with gratitude for something. I know that gratitude will keep you clean, sober, and filled with joy.

TOOL #4: BORROWING AND LENDING

My Christian mentors and church brothers and sisters let me borrow their faith and hope, as I did not have a lot in the beginning. For many wounded people, borrowing faith and hope is all they can do at the beginning of recovery, and even that is a tall order. They have never believed in themselves or seen a future. They have often failed, especially at staying sober. Then they see and hear that Mr. Knuckles believes in them, that I see a successful future for them, and they borrow my faith and hope—just like I did and continue to do when I need to.

Remember in Matthew 14:31 when Peter was walking on water and started to sink? Jesus lifted him up and asked him, "O you of little faith, why did you doubt?" When we are in recovery, we have more doubt about our ability to sink than we have faith to stay afloat. We have little or sometimes no hope for any kind of future. We need others like Jesus to lift us up and remind us not to doubt that God wants us sober, healthy, and whole, and to tell us they see a future for us. Then we can borrow their faith and hope as we develop our own.

As those of us who have faith and hope make ours available to someone in need, it can be uncomfortable for them at first. Those who do not have faith and hope are a suspicious lot! Eventually, as they

WE NEED OTHERS
LIKE JESUS TO LIFT
US UP AND REMIND
US NOT TO DOUBT
THAT GOD WANTS US
SOBER, HEALTHY,
AND WHOLE, AND TO
TELL US THEY SEE A
FUTURE FOR US.

step out more and more, they develop their own faith and hope and are grateful for our sensitivity and care; but for a time, the process of borrowing faith and hope is difficult. They may think we're the crazy ones!

For many of us who have faith and hope, helping someone by letting them borrow our faith and hope can also be outside our comfort zone, even a foreign concept. I've learned over the years that people who have faith and hope need to give theirs away as much as people who don't have those things need to receive them.

Sharing faith and hope is especially powerful when crossing cultures. It breaks down the dividing walls and reveals that whatever our skin color or background, we are all human beings in need of being rescued from our sins. The Bible calls this the "Law of Christ." In other words, it is something Christians do. As we share our faith and hope, everyone in the transaction becomes stronger, more hopeful, filled with faith.

Dear brothers and sisters, if another believer is overcome by some sin, you who are godly should gently and humbly help that person back onto the right path. And be careful not to fall into the same temptation yourself.² Share each other's burdens, and in this way obey the law of Christ.

Galatians 6:1–2 NLT

Jesus said that loving God also meant loving your neighbor:

"And you shall love the Lord your God with all your heart, with all your soul, with all your mind, and with all your strength." This is the first commandment. And the second, like it, is this: "You shall love your neighbor as yourself." There is no other commandment greater than these.

Mark 12:29–31

I submit to you that when it comes to recovery, there is no greater remedy than what you have just read. When you live by these words, you generate the grace and gratitude that both you and others need for recovery. The mixture of your love, faith, and hope is like a high-octane fuel to the people around you, and everyone needs a daily dose! Whether you're lending faith and hope to another or borrowing it from others, you will see the amazing benefits to everyone.

TOOL #5: FAILURE CAN BRING GOOD

Because every recovery path has its share of pitfalls and barriers that present clear and present dangers to progress, both the client and the counselor need help and support. At some point, the counselor will fail, and the one they are trying to help will fail. The biggest hurt is when people you trust betray you. If you don't have support, you might give up.

A good counselor will know and teach that there are valuable lessons in failing. After I realized I could learn from my failures, I made it a habit to ask God, "What am I supposed to learn from this?" Failures provide valuable teaching moments. You can't give up, and at the very least, must trust both the process and people again.

In a staff meeting one day, we were discussing a client who had failed in a position of trust I had assigned him. A colleague said to me braggingly, "Addicts never fool me. I don't trust none of them."

I replied, "I do get fooled sometimes because I trust people. That will never stop me from trusting because I know how important it is to the recovery process. I also know how important that moment of failure is, and how we approach it can determine the outcome."

The other counselor rocked back in his office chair and rubbed his chin. I had gotten him to think more positively about dealing with failure. A counselor can trust and believe in clients more easily when they are not afraid of being betrayed or let down. When they accept the possibility, especially since we are all human, it's much easier to help the client deal with any potential failure. This turns what could have been their undoing into a learning experience that will strengthen them for the future.

TOOL #6: GOD, CLINICIANS, AND FRIENDS

It is extremely difficult, if not impossible, to heal from an emotional setback on your own. I believe people ultimately need God first, then people. I needed a clinician to navigate some of my deeper struggles and failures. Some may need medication to stabilize their mental health. God made these resources available. You must find out how much clinical help you need, then move Heaven and Earth to get it. At the same time, you need a trusted friend who knows you and can help you figure out if the counseling is helping.

God and people are much more available than a clinician, and any good clinician will focus on getting you to the place where you no longer need their services. Still, some of us will need clinical help, and we should never be ashamed or frightened about that! While I was in the Christian rehab program, I asked to go to a secular outpatient program to get more help. I was caught in a loop of suicidal thoughts and temptations to relapse even while my faith in Jesus Christ was growing stronger. I wanted to know more about what was going on with me physically, mentally, and emotionally. This experience not only helped me defeat my demons but gave me the wisdom to help others defeat theirs.

From secular clinicians, I discovered how addiction affected the brain (my brain in particular). An extensive history of alcohol and drug use irreparably damages areas of the brain, as well as the heart, kidneys, liver, lungs, veins, and central nervous system. I found that even my bones were weakened. Things seemed dismal, and this information was a stressor that was hard to overcome. However, I was learning what my challenges were due to years of abusing my body, and they became a point of prayer. I drew upon my faith in God to find my way through.

Again, faith and hope play a vital role in recovery. Whenever I thought about my physical challenges or talked about them with someone, I added, "But Jesus!" I had so much physical damage, my number one hope had to be in Him. The secular clinician was patient with me and my talk about Jesus. Good secular counselors will understand that your faith is your way to maintain hope, which keeps you from relapsing. I had to encourage myself in the Lord, much like David:

Now David was greatly distressed, for the people spoke of stoning him,... But David strengthened himself in the Lord his God.

1 Samuel 30:6

I was abstaining from drugs and alcohol, following the diet and exercising, attending my outpatient support group, and depending on Jesus for a full recovery. I was the oldest and the worst case in our group. There were about ten of us, and most were much younger. I don't know if you know the statistics in addiction and recovery. In the secular clinic, I was one of two who made it through the program. There were over forty men in the Christian center, and I was one of three who made it through.

I believe the difference was Jesus. I was grateful to Him from day one. Then I was grateful for my clinicians, counselors, and friends who helped me see what was really going on with me and what I needed. Anyone who gets sober and stays sober doesn't do it alone. We all need help! We need friends, professionals, and an open and honest relationship with God.

TOOL #7: WORK IS GOOD FOR THE SOUL

Dr. Myles Munroe said, "The wealthiest place on the face of the earth is the cemetery, where lie the visions that were never fulfilled, potentials that were not tapped." It was evil's intent that I should die before I

NOW DAVID WAS GREATLY DISTRESSED, FOR THE PEOPLE SPOKE OF STONING HIM,... BUT DAVID STRENGTHENED HIMSELF IN THE LORD HIS GOD.

1 SAMUEL 30:6

realized my potential and purpose. I thank God that He inspired me to clean those nasty bathrooms! That was the beginning of seeing myself as useful, capable of doing something well that made life easier for others. My reward was self-respect and the thanks of the staff and residents of the recovery center. Then my strong work ethic led to obtaining the job of sexton at the Presbyterian church, where I was also paid. I know that a vital tool in recovery is work. It is good for the soul—and it keeps you out of trouble!

I was so grateful that through such a hard struggle to recover, God blessed me with a job. Now, I see to it that those I help are employed in some kind of work. Job training and getting clients employed were foundational aspects of the Christian program I worked for when I was the director at the center in San Jose, and continues to be foundational as I help others today.

Unfortunately, not all clients are like me. I was always grateful for the job, but some clients just curse the work they are given. Because they haven't learned the value of work, they have no gratitude for it, and their performance on the job suffers. If they don't wise up, they ultimately do something stupid and lose the job. Then their resentment and idleness can lead them to relapse.

The Bible says in John 10:10 that through Jesus Christ we have abundant life, but that doesn't mean we get saved, sit on clouds all day, and God drops everything we need from Heaven. It says in James 2:14–18 that true faith leads to acts of faith. For a client beginning in recovery, we must find something they can do. With God's help, they will eventually be working at something they enjoy doing that gives them great satisfaction and joy as well as financial resources.

One of the biggest ways to help someone in recovery is to assist them in employment. I have learned that by training others or facilitating a client's training, their gratitude will inspire them to pass that help on to others. We help others so that they can help others. *That* is the abundant life God gives us. Seeing others gain confidence and self-esteem by earning their living and providing for their families is a source of joy. And we can never stop! If we stop helping others, trouble is just around the corner.

People who understand the value of their work and are grateful for it are the happiest people I know. A day filled with thanks for the grace of God to do a good day's work is a day worth living. This gratitude brings out your best and brings your best to your day. Recovery is not only discovering who you are but also finding out what you were born to do. Those who find their purpose and carry out that purpose are far less likely to relapse, knowing they have so much to live for now.

CHAPTER SIXTEEN

MONEY AND STEWARDSHIP

Money is a big issue for the addict or alcoholic because they need money to buy their drug of choice. Therefore, money takes on a very powerful meaning. In recovery, they have to learn an entirely different attitude toward money and how to manage it. I teach the biblical view, which promotes inner peace.

The Bible says in 1 Timothy 6:10 that the love of money is the root of all evil. Money itself is not evil, but the love of it, or depending on it more than God, will lead to all kinds of evil. For an addict like me, money was a trigger. I can remember conversations I would have with myself about money. "Now, I'm only going to spend a little of this money, and I'm going to do the right thing with the rest."

Then the money would say, "But I'm here, and you can have what you want. You know you don't want to stop spending! Especially when things are good." That was a battle I couldn't win.

For a lot of addicts, money is a trigger. I've seen them get large sums of money from a settlement or an inheritance, and they would take it and either overdose or get killed by another addict who stole their money. Time and again, I saw how a large sum of money was the death of an addict. I've seen functional addicts wither away to skin and bone or lose their minds because they could continuously make money. I've read about experiments where rats literally starved to death right next to a plate of food because they were given a never-ending supply of cocaine. Addiction is a wicked, evil thing, and it is fueled by the love of money.

When I was using, I worked very hard at my jobs. The irony is that because it was obvious I was a desperate addict, I was never paid fairly. They knew I would take every penny of what little they paid me and give it to a dealer. In my sick mind, money meant only one thing: drugs. In a sense, money was the god who gave me an escape from my pain.

I would give my hard-earned money to drug dealers, many of whom did not like me and tried to humiliate me. Some dealers are just mean. After all, they are selling something that destroys lives, families, and communities. They are either an addict themselves, greedy beyond reason or drunk with power over addicts—like the dealers who shot me in the head for fun. I once saw a dealer make a young, addicted girl eat a dead cockroach for a five-dollar crack rock. He and another dealer were competing over who could get an addict to do the most humiliating thing. Some of the things I saw them do are too terrible to mention here.

BANKS?!

Once God got me out of addiction and into recovery, I began to work as a responsible man. I earned money and began to value it in a good way. When Christians told me early on that every good and perfect gift comes from the Father (James 1:17), I saw money differently. I knew that my job and my paycheck came from Him.

One day, I was talking to a volunteer who told me they needed the first floor of their house painted. After prayer one evening, my good friend Jerry and I hatched a plan to start our own painting company.

We had no family, so on weekends, we painted houses. Jerry was a professional painter, and I was a pretty good manager who could paint. We just did interiors, but we were good. Working almost straight through the weekend, we could paint a whole downstairs or upstairs and sometimes both.

The first house Jerry and I painted, we did a great job in record time. The volunteer was so delighted, she spread the word to other people in her neighborhood. Once the quality of our work got around, we had more work than we could wish for. At the end of the weekend, when we came back to the rehab, we would go to our lockers when no one else was around. We would put our money in our 12 x 12 lockers, which were meant for books. Since we weren't living with the most honest people, we kept this our secret. If anyone found out, the money would disappear.

I was a careful saver, but I had never used a bank. As a homeless addict, I had hidden my money in floorboards, abandoned buildings, and under mattresses. Banks were a foreign concept to me. Our painting business did well, and eventually I had saved $10,000! Bursting with pride, I just had to tell someone.

The next time Russ came to visit, I had the "cat who ate the canary" look on my face. I took him into the cafeteria, where we sat on a bench facing the lockers. No one else was there, so we could speak privately. Russ asked, "What's up with you today?"

I lowered my voice to a whisper, "Russ, don't look now but do you see that locker 127?"

Russ replied, "Yes. What's the matter with you? Why are you whispering?"

"Shhh, not too loud. People might hear."

"Hear what?" Russ asked.

"I've got a huge secret to tell you. Just act like we're just talking."

"Well, we are just talking. What?"

"Can you see over my shoulder, locker 127? Don't stare! Just glance at it sort of incognito and don't draw attention."

"Okay, Charles, what's going on?"

I giggled, "I've saved $10,000, and it's in that locker, and my friend Jerry has $7,000 in the one next to it."

Russ's face looked like when a car breaks full stop. "You've got ten grand in that flimsy locker?"

"Yeah, isn't that cool?"

"No, Charles. You need to put that money in the bank."

Everything went quiet. My mind raced. Had I made a mistake trusting Russ? I didn't use banks. I hid my money from everyone. Didn't he know that banks have nothing to do with people like me? "Come on, Russ. Would a bank take *my* money?"

Russ laughed. It was the kind of laugh that says you're better than you think you are. "Charles, of course a bank will take your money." He told me a bank would take my money and give it back to me when I wanted it. He explained how to set up a checking account. In those moments, I struggled to get past my perspective on money and banks from thirty years of addiction. I had belonged in the outer edges of society, but now Russ was challenging not only what I believed about banks, but what I had believed about myself.

THE RIGHT WAY TO SEE MONEY

When I walked into the bank to set up my new account, I was fully prepared to be rejected. To my shock, the teller smiled when I handed her the neatly stacked money—like she was impressed! Not long after, I walked out with my new bankbook and checks. I felt like my feet weren't touching the ground. I was floating.

After becoming a licensed counselor, I told my clients how I had to change my outlook on banks and see money in a different way, the right way. I told them that before I started using direct deposit, I would put my check on the table and ask God, "What do You want me to do with this money?" There were two things He let me know from my time in the Christian rehab program and with Russ: 1) put the money in the bank, then it won't bother you, and you won't bother it; 2) give, to your church and charities. Of course, I paid my rent, insurance, gas, and food; but following this new discipline, my bank account grew, and my relationship with money was fully subject to my relationship with God.

Today, I wonder what would have happened if the wrong person had discovered my money and stolen it. How would I have responded? What would that have done to me, to my recovery? If I hadn't put my money in the bank and had kept it on me, what would I have done, especially late at night or facing a hard challenge? I was blessed that God had given me a good counselor to point me in the right direction.

Russ helped me to understand that money is not only to meet my needs but to help others. By using my money to make a difference in someone else's life, I realized more and more that money is a neutral commodity. As long as I love God and use money in His service, my life is good.

THE RIGHT WAY TO SPEND MONEY

After giving to my church and paying my bills, I considered what to do with my money. I'm not a big movie fan or a fast food freak, and I had stopped smoking when I gave my life to Jesus. To keep from spending my money on my addiction again, I found "healthy splurges." One of my biggest splurges was taking the men I sponsored in AA to a wonderful dinner after the Friday night meeting. Most of the time, they would just get pie and coffee, but some would eat a meal if they were really hungry. We would read from the AA *Big Book* and talk.

I'll call one of the men I sponsored Mark. He was a business analyst, a world traveler, had a sizable income, and was a cultured person. Our paths would never cross in the real world—but in the world of addiction, we were on a level playing field. At first, sponsoring Mark was a bit awkward. I cleaned floors, and he flew to different countries to advise huge businesses. Mark wanted to pay when we talked at the diner because he was financially better off than me, but I would pick up the check. Finally, he asked me, "How can I repay you when you won't let me pick up the tab?"

I said, "Mark, you will repay me when you do this for the person you sponsor."

I've lost count of the men I sponsored in AA over the years. Without exception, they would be grateful and ask, "How can I pay you back?"

I would say, "Do this for someone else."

Money was no longer a means for evil in my life; it was now a means for good. It was in the bank, and God and I controlled it; it did not control me. In finding good ways to spend my money, I learned the joy of giving.

SOWING AND REAPING

When I started the cleaning service, for which I hired guys in recovery, I also instituted a time of dedication. Every payday, we all put our checks on the table and dedicated them to God in prayer. I always give this advice to recovering addicts: "It's not yours, it's God's. Act like it." In other words, pray about how you spend the money and have a good attitude about where you are led to put it. Whether you're paying a bill, giving an offering at your church, or feeding the homeless, take joy in using what God has given you to be a blessing to others.

I've also noticed another phenomenon. I cannot prove this, but it has proved itself true in my life and many others. When I give to the church and other charities, my money grows. I believe that it all belongs to God, and we are only stewards of His wealth. If we use what He gives us wisely and according to His will, then He will take care of us financially:

> Seek the Kingdom of God above all else, and live righteously, and he will give you everything you need.

Matthew 6:33 NLT

SEEK THE KINGDOM OF GOD ABOVE ALL ELSE, AND LIVE RIGHTEOUSLY, AND HE WILL GIVE YOU EVERYTHING YOU NEED.

MATTHEW 6:33 NLT

A Wise Choice of Home

One of the biggest relapse triggers is money, so it's a very important conversation in relapse prevention. The first and main condition was that the client is totally transparent with you concerning their finances. If they are cagey or acting suspicious, then they may be in partial recovery or moving toward relapse.

A big part of money management has to do with where the client lives. As I have said before, when I moved out of the rehab, no one guided me; so, I moved back to my old neighborhood, right next to my old abandominium. The day I moved in, some of the same addicts were on the steps next door, looking at me. I knew they were taking inventory of my stuff, as burglars do.

After work, instead of going home to my depressing room in a depressing neighborhood, I volunteered at the homeless shelter, went to AA meetings, and attended a Bible study. Every night, I went home expecting my room to be burglarized.

One evening, I had to stay a little later at the mission because of an incident. One of the volunteer barbers had accidentally shaved an eyebrow off one of the shelter guests! It looked funny, but it was no time for laughter. The shelter guest wanted revenge. I talked him out of a fistfight and convinced him to let the barber shave off the other eyebrow and finish the haircut. All was well, and I headed home.

As I pulled up to park, out of the shadows came a hunched-over figure. His hand was at his beltline, and I knew he had a gun. I had already turned off my engine, so I froze, bending over the steering wheel. Both my hands were on the wheel, and I wasn't going to make any sudden moves. I prayed the gunman was a professional stickup man and not a scary amateur who might shoot me. While I was stuck in that position, a group of cars turned the corner, and their headlights lit up the street. The gunman pushed his gun back down, and I turned the key to the ignition and burned rubber down the street.

At this time, my friend Russ and I had an informal relationship, but he did say I could call him anytime. The next morning, I called. "Russ, they almost got me last night."

"Charles, what are you talking about? Who are they?"

"I got a room on 9th street, and coming home last night, I almost got robbed. It was a miracle that I got away."

"You moved back to that area? Why?"

"Russ, where else am I going to live?"

"Charles, you can live in a nicer neighborhood if you want. Why not move to Media?"

"Russ, they gonna let me live in Media? Come on now," I laughed.

"Sure, Charles. And with the job you have, you can afford it."

Russ was challenging me to see myself differently again. I thought about it, and then I talked to the director of the program. He told me he would call a friend who owned some apartments in the area. I went to see his friend, and I got a studio right in Media, Pennsylvania. It only took me a few hours to move in because I didn't have many belongings. I finished late in the evening, laid on the floor, and thanked God.

Later, I got up and went out on the front steps, and sat. I noticed an older couple. They were walking casually and holding hands, then went into the donut shop across the street. Out of impulse, I wanted to run after them and warn them not to be out so late. Through the window, I saw them sit down and enjoy a donut in each other's company. As I watched them, I thought, *I'm not in the ghetto anymore. This is how people live in freedom. Thank you, Lord!*

Where a client lives and what they call home is important. If they live in a depressed area, there is more of a chance for relapse. Many are going to need financial coaching to live in a nicer, safer neighborhood. That is another reason I encourage them to become part of a church family, ministry, or program that can help them until they can earn enough to support themselves. This encourages responsibility. Also, if they live in a nice place, they will experience more gratitude, and gratitude fuels recovery.

We must never love money! And we must always use it to fulfill the will of God. This keeps us healthy and full of joy as we use our resources to take good care of ourselves and help others.

CHAPTER SEVENTEEN
MAINTAINING GOOD HEALTH

When clients start to get their physical health back, they can go to an extreme. I've seen some clients become obsessed with their physical shape. They focus on bodybuilding to the detriment of everything else. They move past healthy supplements to anabolic steroids, which become their new drug of choice. They reason with themselves that this is a good thing, that they are staying strong.

This move to an extreme is hard for a counselor to catch. Their client looks healthy and appears to have a healthy outlet, and supplements and steroids do not show on toxicology screen panels used to detect drugs. They cannot see a corrupted and partial recovery. Aside from spiritually discerning that something is wrong, one of the signs is that the client becomes increasingly selfish and self-centered. They no longer operate in an attitude of gratitude to God and those who support them in recovery.

Don't Trade Addictions

Some clients regain good physical health and develop a sex addiction. This is more easily detected by a counselor and friends in recovery. I also remember one client who had a wicked cigarette habit. Even though he was sober, his obsession with cigarettes would get him into trouble. Clients need to be taught their emotional and mental triggers for addiction and understand that if those triggers aren't dismantled, they can be sober and develop another addiction.

One facilitator dealt with cigarette addiction this way. As he was ending the class, he said, "Most of us are going to pray to God. But for you men waiting for the class to end so that you can smoke," and he pulled out a cigarette and balanced it on the end of the table, "you can pray to this cigarette because that's your god."

A friend of mine who was a heavy smoker rose up with fire in his eyes and shouted, "I ain't gonna pray to no damn cigarette! That ain't my God!" Strangely enough, he did not go out to smoke with the other men, and to this day, he has never smoked again. One could explain this as being some brilliant therapeutic tactic, and they would be partially right, but here's where the spiritual element made the difference: My friend never went to AA 12-Step meetings or asked for an AA sponsor, but he did have spiritual mentors. After rehab, he never drank or smoked again, went on to become a minister, and we remain friends today.

Another client who smoked for decades was having problems with cigarettes in his early sobriety. I suggested that he might consider if he had an oral fixation and had to put something in his mouth. This thought alarmed him, so he never smoked again. This man also wanted desperately to please God.

These wonderful victories often happen against the advice of fellow clinicians. They comfort clients by telling them how difficult it is to quit smoking and advise them not to worry about that addiction. Just face one addiction at a time. Contrary to this well-intentioned counsel, I have found that people who continue their smoking addiction are usually more vulnerable to other addictions and relapse.

Again, the counselor has to encourage the client to get to the root of all their problems to eliminate all harmful addictions. Jesus gave a perfect illustration of this:

> *"When an unclean spirit goes out of a man, he goes through dry places, seeking rest; and finding none, he says, 'I will return to my house from which I came.' And when he comes, he finds it swept and put in order. Then he goes and takes with him seven other spirits more wicked than himself, and they enter and dwell there; and the last state of that man is worse than the first."*
>
> *And it happened, as He spoke these things, that a certain woman from the crowd raised her voice and said to Him, "Blessed is the womb that bore You, and the breasts which nursed You!"*
>
> *But He said, "More than that, blessed are those who hear the word of God and keep it!"*

Luke 11:24–28

Jesus said that we could only stay free by hearing God's Word and then living by it. That's what my two brothers in the Lord and I did. We each said, "Cigarettes are not my god!" We cast that addiction demon out of our lives, and then we filled ourselves with God's Word, the bread of life. When the demon came back to tempt us, the Word in our hearts gave us the strength to say no. Our body may have wanted to relapse for a moment, but our spirit rose and told the demon and our body to shut up!

Spiritually, I recognize the reality of one addiction leaving the door open to others. Eventually, the addictive personality will go with what is most familiar and adopt other addictions or relapse into the primary one. To avoid this, I teach the men how their addictive tendency can jump from one addiction to another, how demons can suggest, "Oh, that looks good. Let's concentrate on that. After all, it's not your addiction." The idea is to recognize the addictive tendency when it surfaces and reject it, shut the demons up, and continue in a healthy, complete recovery.

One Bite at a Time

When I entered recovery, I had severe physical problems. Even so, I began to get stronger. Jack was a former pro football player who came to the center just about every day. He would drive us to appointments and take a couple of us shopping for food. But the most wonderful thing he did was take us on walks in the park. Sometimes he took us to a big college field with a track. I had severe respiratory issues, so I would dread it. I knew I couldn't run the quarter-mile track. It just looked daunting. So I gave Jack trouble. I was afraid I would fail, and I didn't need another failure. But this was not Jack's first rodeo, and he was a gentle Christian giant. Instead of embarrassing me until I would break and give up, he would sit with me after he ran his quarter-mile. I would complain to him, "I can't do it, Jack, so I ain't gonna."

He would say, "Well, Charles, you came all the way out here; you might as well do something." I told him that I didn't want to embarrass myself in front of all the other men. I didn't want to lose their respect. Jack replied, "Charles, you can't lose their respect if you have enough respect for yourself. Just give it a try. Don't think about running the quarter-mile; just try walking as far as you can and then sit for a while and try again."

Jack was a world-class coach. In the following weeks, I walked the quarter-mile, and then I walked a half-mile. Before I knew it, I was running a half-mile and running it happily. Again, Bishop Tutu's quote came to mind, "How do you eat an elephant? One bite at a time." It also reminded me of my days as *The Flash*. My heart still desired to run fast!

More than regaining the ability to run, Jack gave me a living example of coaching others by teaching and being a role model. That is why, right after I graduated from the program, I came back as a volunteer to help other men learn these valuable lessons—and took the men on hikes! When I became a director in San Jose, I obtained a bunch of bikes. Many were junk, but my buddy Mark put together a bike room and started a bike repair class. He made every bike a fine-tuned machine. Soon, we had enough bikes to take all the men on a ride. I was in my

60s, but I showed up in gratitude to Jack, passing on everything he taught me.

One day, we were hiking up a huge hill in a state park. Just as we approached the summit, one of the more smarty-pants, comedic guys stopped and said, "Wait a minute. Hold up just a second." Everyone looked at him as if to ask why, and he said, "Quiet, listen to Mr. Knuckles' breathing." Everyone, including myself, cracked up laughing. The park was so quiet, and all anyone could hear was my breathing in and out.

I said, "I breathe hard, but I won't stop." I continued to bike hills and climb mountains with them, and God's grace would propel me past my limitations. They seemed to like that. I was real. I was limited and vulnerable, but I loved them enough to be there for them. I showed them that if I could do it, they could do it.

Jesus said to him, "Thomas, because you have seen Me, you have believed. Blessed are those who have not seen and yet have believed."

John 20:29

Most people look down on Thomas in the Bible. We call him "Doubting Thomas." The truth is, we are all doubting Thomases! Thomas had to see the scars on Jesus' hands, feet, and side before he would believe. With this in mind, I practice a kind of wounded warrior counseling for men and their families. I'm fully transparent and vulnerable with them. I don't just open my shirt and show my wounds; I work with my shirt off so that my wounds can be a constant reminder of just how great and loving our God is. I've learned that vulnerability shows them real strength, God's saving power.

Most addicts are Thomases. They have to see your wounds, to put their fingers in the holes of your past and the dark places you still fight to conquer. That's how we all heal. This vulnerability is one of the reasons why AA is the leading resource in recovery. It's a bunch of wounded healers healing each other through brutal honesty and love. We all need to see Jesus set someone free in order to believe He can set us free too.

JESUS SAID TO HIM, "THOMAS, BECAUSE YOU HAVE SEEN ME, YOU HAVE BELIEVED. BLESSED ARE THOSE WHO HAVE NOT SEEN AND YET HAVE BELIEVED."

JOHN 20:29

NUTRITION

Eating good food and drinking enough water is important for every human being, so these things are crucial for those in recovery. Many books have covered good nutrition, so I won't say a lot on the topic. However, I do wish to stress again that nicotine intake in any form is never good. Most clinics think this habit is too hard to stop, especially while trying to stay sober. I disagree. I think it is critical for your health and complete recovery to stop smoking without using nicotine pills, chewing nicotine gum, or vaping. They are another addiction, not recovery, and the damage from these forms of nicotine will weaken your resolve and your body, making relapse more of a possibility.

Smoking of any kind damages the oxygen intake process. This is important for many reasons, the most important being that the brain needs oxygen to think clearly. Clear thoughts help recovery. I lament not being able to keep up with the physical activities I love now that I'm sober, primarily because of how much I smoked. Lamenting is a very important term for the recovering addict because it is so closely linked to depression. Smoking can exacerbate depression, and that is something a smoker must consider in recovery.

The Bible calls the body of the Christian "the temple of the Holy Spirit" (1 Corinthians 6:19). Our body is the house where the Holy Spirit resides. Think of your body as a large temple of stone. Then imagine excessive nicotine, caffeine, and sugar weakening your foundation. What strengthens your temple: A good diet consisting of fish, poultry, fruits, and vegetables, while avoiding processed foods. Also, plenty of fresh air, sun, and exercise. These things are essential for recovery. Our minds work at their optimum when our bodies are working at their optimum. Any program that does not cover these things as pathways out of bad habits is shortchanging their clients.

Once, I took the men to a retreat in the mountains. We drove up the steep inclines on narrow roads. We were so happy to get out of the city, and the mountain views made us thank God for His many wonders. Suddenly, something just told me to pull over and look. We stopped, and just as we walked to the edge to look out over the valley, rocks came tumbling down behind us, stopping just short of the road. It quickened our breaths, and as we turned to look upon the majestic view, we knew we should give thanks to God.

Later, when we arrived at the camp, we were famished. We unloaded the vans and headed to the cafeteria. On the way, there was a fountain. I stopped to take a drink. This water tasted sweeter than any water I had tasted before. I knew if I had not been in recovery and quit smoking, I would have never tasted the sweetness of the water or stopped to see God's glory. My obsession with getting a fix or a smoke would have ruined all that.

The Bible says the little foxes spoil the vine, meaning it's usually not a big event that triggers a relapse; it is all the little things that we let slide, that we don't face and deal with. The little things add up to cause us to stumble and fall, so we want to make sure we don't let anything that looks small get past us. That small thing can turn into a relapse.

Eat good food. Drink water. Exercise your body and your brain. Refuse to smoke or fall into any other habits that could be harmful and addictive. Be honest and vulnerable with God and those who support you. Doing these things will enrich every part of your life: at home, at work, at meetings, and spending time with good friends. Each of these things seems little and insignificant, but over time, they add up to something significant: maintaining good health.

CHAPTER EIGHTEEN
MASTERING THE MUNDANE

Addicts are very familiar with the extreme highs and lows of the addictive lifestyle. As crazy as it sounds, these become our comfort zones. When things are really bad, we learn to adapt. We don't consider stopping using but work all the harder to get loaded again. We know that at the end of all our hard work, we will be rewarded with drugs or alcohol. Our behavior is locked in an addictive mentality, burning neural pathways into our brain. We're trapped physically, mentally, socially, and spiritually. The addictive agent, whatever it may be, appears to be our savior. Over time, we become obsessed and easily adjust to the chaos in which we live. We cannot conceive a normal life. Within ourselves, we do not have the power to adjust to "normalcy."

One of the greatest dangers recovering addicts must face is the mundane. We have no comprehension of a status quo, a normal life, or the daily schedule. We have to learn about this phenomenal way of living and begin to practice it in our recovery. Eventually, we will experience the joy of a day well spent and never want to depart from the mundane, the ordinary. For an addict, mastering the mundane becomes an extraordinary miracle—but it only happens through faith in God and hard work.

THE PAIN OF SOBRIETY

To master the mundane, the recovering addict must first understand something called "the pain of sobriety." It's part of the mental health component. If an addict is without their addictive agent, the first pain is physical—but when physical withdrawal ceases, they face the inner pain of withdrawal. They begin to see themselves with clear eyes, are flooded with memories they used to escape, feel overwhelmed by emotions they can't navigate, and their body and central nervous system are damaged. It is the pain of sobriety, and if not handled correctly, the addict will relapse.

An addict has been programmed to get rid of the pain by using their drug of choice. They have no concept of dealing with pain any other way. They certainly can't see any comfort in the mundane, and the pain of sobriety erupts strongest in the midst of it. When the mind is relaxed, our most practiced thoughts will present the strongest. "I'm bored. Nothing good is happening. It's too quiet. Where's the party? I need something to make me feel good. I feel so low. I need to get high!" Then all the bad memories come flooding in to reinforce the fact that we need something to make the nightmare stop.

Our average dreams are hard to remember, but our nightmares are memorable. Whatever drove us to addiction seems scarier because of the years we spent running away from it. To the sober mind, these horrors are magnified, especially in the unguarded moments of the mundane. It is in these unguarded moments that many relapses happen.

This phenomenon is called "the unguarded moment," the "strange mental blank spot," or the "unconscious movement toward relapse." Either way, our condition is the same. We must be trained for these mundane moments, ready to make the unconscious conscious.

PITTSBURGH BOB

In early recovery, I went to three or four AA meetings per week. One meeting was called "The Dry Dock." A friend said to me, "You've got to get to know the guy who is speaking tonight." I nodded and interpreted this to mean that I should make more sober friends. We took our seats, and the speaker of the night sauntered to the table. He was wearing an old straw cowboy hat, with the brim rolled up and coming to a point at the front. He wore the most elaborate cowboy boots I'd ever seen, faded jeans, and a flannel shirt. We were in one of the most urban sections of Philly, so I turned to my friend and said, "You want me to be friends with him?"

He just smiled and said, "Sure. Just wait. Listen to him."

I leaned back, folded my arms, and my body language told my thoughts: *Ain't no way.*

Then the cowboy told his story. It was just like mine! He ran through his childhood and then his "drunkalog." He got sober, and after eight years of sobriety, he had a great job, had gotten married and had kids, and they lived in a nice house. One day he got an invitation to his high school reunion. He sat down with his old friends and started reminiscing. It turned into a belly-laughing, knee-slapping good time. A waitress came over and set up the table with drinks, and in the middle of a huge laugh, he picked up the drink and drank it. One drink is too many and a thousand is not enough for the alcoholic. Fast forward. He lost his job, then his house, then his wife and kids. It would be six years before he managed to get sober again.

He talked about how he got sober again in God, how good God had been to him, and how good sobriety is. He ended with, "My name is Pittsburg Bob, and thanks for letting me share."

I thought, *Oh, my goodness! I've got to meet Pittsburg Bob!* Everybody surrounded him to shake his hand or get a hug. I waited patiently, and the more I saw him interact with people, the more I knew he had to be my friend. When we did become friends, we talked again about that unguarded moment when he picked up that drink.

A few years later, I was invited to an event in the Pocono mountains. We had a great time. In the evening, there was a huge celebration. We were seated at our table laughing when the waitress started setting glasses of champagne next to each of us. Right in the middle of a great laugh, my hand reached over to pick up my drink. My brain said, "Whoa, Pittsburg Bob." I called the waitress and asked her to take the glasses away, explaining that this was a non-alcohol table and we were celebrating our sobriety. Because of my friend, whom I'd listened to in a meeting, I turned an unguarded moment into one that was guarded. The story of Pittsburg Bob saved the day for me and everyone at that table.

> *Be anxious for nothing, but in everything by prayer and supplication, with thanksgiving, let your requests be made known to God; and the peace of God, which surpasses all understanding, will guard your hearts and minds through Christ Jesus.*

> *Philippians 4:6–7*

When we have an unguarded moment, this passage of Scripture promises that the peace of God will guard our hearts and minds. The Holy Spirit in us will give us a nudge and say, "Pittsburg Bob!"

WHY AM I BORED?

Do not mistake the mundane for boredom. Recovering addicts tend to say, "I'm bored." The main reason why we are "bored," especially in early recovery, is because we are boring! I didn't have much of a life in addiction. I lived to use drugs and used drugs to live. If you did a time-lapse photography video of my life, it would be like the movie *Groundhog Day*—the same thing happening every day but without real comfort or beauty.

Boredom is not the life God has for us. When we are bored, we are not living for Him but for ourselves. We are looking to other people and things to make us feel good, satisfy us and meet our needs. In John 10:10, Jesus said that He came to give us abundant life. When we live our life for Him, we find out we are never bored! We are either discovering new revelations in God's Word or putting it into practice, having adventures of faith as we do what He's instructed us to do—and He usually asks us to do things that require great faith!

Normal life may seem boring after being conditioned for years to live in highs and lows, anything close to "normal" is considered boring, but that is an evil deception. The truth is that the addict's life is sickeningly boring, especially the lows. In the lows we are sick, starved for life, and deceived to believe that the drug is life, that what is killing us is fun. We have been duped into believing what is false and reject the truth. The truth is that we are wasting our lives in the most boring way.

When we get into recovery and begin to live for a Heavenly Father who loves us and knows us better than anyone else, life becomes colorful and amazing like we could never have imagined. After all, this is the God who parted the Red Sea. There is nothing boring about Him!

THE MUNDANE CANVAS

Addicts give up the life they were created to live for the life they imagine with their addictions. The truth is that our mundane is God's blank canvas. As we recover, fully surrendered to the God who made us and knows what's best for us, we become His masterpiece. With Him, we paint a miraculous new life, a life we never dreamed possible. The mundane brings forth our best life, the greatest adventure, fulfilling our deepest desires in true freedom.

How do we do this? We start by putting a high value on the mundane. The world, our flesh, and the devil will do their best to convince us that the mundane is an undesirable place to exist, so we must train ourselves to dispel that lie. We were not created to be constantly entertained. We were made to create things and do things that honor and serve God, that are good for us and for others.

Mastering the mundane is mastering every level of life, the daily routine of eating, working, being with friends and family, sleeping, fun, and adventure. The key is to see the supposedly mundane in its true light. Take breathing, for example. It is a common, mundane habit, but our life would quickly change if we couldn't breathe! As a former smoker, taking a deep, clean breath is a joy for me. When we see the mundane as a canvas upon which our lives are painted in vibrant, life-giving colors, that mundane habit or task becomes something beautiful, even miraculous; instead of being bored, we are incredibly grateful.

We can say the same about eating, working, sleeping, and all other daily routines. They are blessings. Every sip of clean water or bite of bread, project at work, talk with a friend, and good night's sleep—becomes beautiful and precious. In this way, we see the merciful and gracious hand of God in everything we experience. If we stop seeing Him and stop doing life with Him, then the mundane turns dark again, becoming a chore. Instead of being grateful, we become frustrated, anxious, and even bitter.

The only thing that will bring the color back to our mundane canvas is dying to ourselves and living for Jesus Christ, for the God who saved us, healed us, and set us free. He is the master artist.

NEVER THE SAME

Mastering the mundane and entering into the miracle of it takes effort and support. We must be intentional about gratitude in every little good thing in our lives, from the air we breathe to a restored marriage. When a person cannot generate gratitude, evil gains a foothold, and relapse can sneak up on them. And, there is something else now. After an addict has experienced sobriety and the miracle of the mundane, acting on their addiction is not the same. They have seen the possibility of a different and better life. They have truth running around in their heads, fighting the lies that want to destroy them. After being sober, the addict who returns to their addiction is in more pain and misery than

WE MUST BE INTENTIONAL ABOUT GRATITUDE IN EVERY LITTLE GOOD THING IN OUR LIFE, FROM THE AIR WE BREATHE TO A RESTORED MARRIAGE.

they were before they experienced sobriety—because now they know the difference.

Sometimes a relapse will shine the light on how mundane moments are miraculous gifts from God, little hints of His steadfast love and infinite care. People who relapse after being sober then wish for the mundane! To eat, sleep, wake up and read their Bible, go to work, come home to enjoy their family, plan epic vacations, and the daily adventure of walking with Jesus is a miracle, the joyous miracle of the mundane.

You don't master the mundane in your own strength but as you submit to the Lord in your daily routine. The hardest work is deciding to go through what you need to go through to get there! Then He goes through it with you, building you up in every step you take. He makes you smarter and opens your eyes to things you never saw before. The mundane is His gift to you, His reward for trusting Him; it is where you find His grace, peace, joy, and restoration.

As we find joy in these not-so-small blessings, we become more intimate with our Heavenly Father. We get to know Him better. We know ourselves and others better. We discover that He makes what the world calls the mundane miraculous and extraordinary—and we enter the joy of days well spent.

A FINAL WORD

Only Jesus can take all the broken pieces of our lives and make us whole. As we say in recovery:

The bad news is, we can't heal ourselves.

The good news is that He can.

The question is, will we let Him?

Death is coming for the addict, and you are in a battle for your life. Use every tool available to fight, because you may not get a second chance. Don't give up on yourself! Looking back over my life, I could say that there was no one there for me, but that isn't true. God was. He rescued me 100 times before I knew Him. The 101st time, my eyes finally opened, and I realized I was rescued by Him. When I look back on recovery, I see that God cared enough to keep rescuing me, that He continues to rescue me at this very moment and He sent many others to help me.

I remember how I went from foster home to foster home, and no one adopted me. Then one day, God did. The Creator of the Universe moved Heaven and Earth to rescue me and adopt me as His precious son. All I had to do was grab hold of His hand. I don't even have to worry about letting go, because I don't want to! And I know that if I do begin to lose my grip, He will tighten His. He will never let me go. He loves me no matter what happens, and He has given me a wife and friends who aspire to be just like Him. When someone loves you that much, it's easy to give them your whole being, your whole life.

My counselors told me that my recovery was up to me. I could put a little into it or I could put a lot into it. I figured Jesus died and put everything He had into me, so I was going to put everything I had into serving Him in my recovery. If you want to help broken people become whole and help yourself at the same time, help people to see Jesus in you and to know Jesus through you.

Your friend and servant: Charles Lee Knuckles, Redeemed.

I can do all things through Christ, who strengthens me.

Philippians 4:13

I CAN DO ALL THINGS THROUGH CHRIST, WHO STRENGTHENS ME.

PHILIPPIANS 4:13

ABOUT THE AUTHOR

Charles Lee Knuckles is a Licensed Advanced Alcohol and Drug Counselor and formerly the Director of the CityTeam San Jose Rescue Mission and Recovery Center. He has spent the last 22 years serving men from "Jail to Yale" who walk through his door seeking help, and he does not turn away a soul. He's happily married and lives in Surfside Beach, South Carolina.

FOR MORE INFORMATION AND
RESOURCES, PLEASE VISIT

WWW.CHARLESKNUCKLES.COM